RIDE

JOSH KENCH

RIDE

FROM ULTRA-CYCLING ROOKIE
TO RACING ACROSS AMERICA

ALLEN&UNWIN

SYDNEY・MELBOURNE・AUCKLAND・LONDON

Allen & Unwin
Sydney, Melbourne, Auckland, London

Level 3, 228 Queen Street
Auckland 1010, New Zealand
Phone: (64 9) 377 3800

83 Alexander Street
Crows Nest NSW 2065, Australia
Phone: (61 2) 8425 0100
Email: info@allenandunwin.com
Web: www.allenandunwin.com

National Library of New Zealand Cataloguing-in-Publication Data

Kench, Joshua, 1972-
Ride : from ultra-cycling rookie to racing across America / Joshua
Kench, Kerry Jimson.
ISBN 978-1-877505-15-7
1. Kench, Joshua, 1972- 2. Bicycle racing. I. Jimson, Kerry.
II. Title.
796.62092—dc 23

ISBN 978 1 877505 15 7

Set in 13.5/17.5 pt Adobe Garamond Pro by Midland Typesetters, Australia
Printed and bound in Australia by Griffin Press

10 9 8 7 6 5 4 3 2 1

Contents

'Those who do it, can't explain. Those
who don't do it, don't understand.'
Peter Cole

Chapter 1

Jumping in the saddle

The people trapped beneath the bitumen clawed at the underside. The road had become transparent, like black ice – hot black ice. They struggled, scraping with their fingernails, trying to claw their way out.

I swerved. From the following support vehicle, via my plug-in earphone, a voice told me to 'pedal, pedal, pedal'. But the faces! I couldn't ride straight over them, slice them with my wheels. They glared at me – faces from a horror film, people escaping the underworld, under a sheet of molten tar and stones.

I told myself to ride on, keep going. They're not really there. It's sleep deprivation. It's days of nonstop cycling. It's the headlights from the follow vehicle casting weird shadows across the road.

1

But when the dark hallucinations take hold, you can't ignore them. They're as real as any night terror. The race becomes a fight with yourself to keep going, to push through the nightmare images. Your support crew struggles to keep you focused, to point you in the right direction. Just to keep you on your bike.

The tyres rolled over the desperate, accusing eyes. Keep going, keep going . . .

But I'm getting ahead of myself.

Everyone in the Race Across America (RAAM) fights the dark images when they've been awake long enough. They also fight profound exhaustion, extreme pain, dizzying disorientation, raw bodies and even death itself.

And the hallucinations? They're bad. But they're only part of the mind games in this ultra-contest.

If I back-pedal ten years, I can trace to when the RAAM really started for me. Back to when I got into this compelling, addictive madness called enduro sports. It started at my brother's wedding.

∽∞∾

Kane and Jan got married in Palmerston North's Rose Garden and held the reception at the Cloverlea Tavern. It was after the speeches and supper and a few whiskies and beers. I was having a cigarette and told the friends and family who were seated at the table that I was going to do the Coast to Coast.

As endurance races go, this is pretty hardcore. It's a multi-sport competition, with a course that is spectacular, beautiful and gruelling. It starts off at Kumara Beach on the west coast of the South Island. Competitors cycle, run and kayak 243 kilometres to Sumner Beach on the other side of the island.

Jump right in. That was my attitude. Have a crack. How hard can it be? Isn't that the Kiwi way? It's said that New Zealanders do things because they haven't learned that they can't, right? Those mental roadblocks and self-imposed limitations aren't there. We've got a fresh eye and a can-do attitude.

Whatever the truth of that, there's an impulsive urge in me. A voice that says, go on. Don't over-think it. If you start thinking about it, you'll see all the obstacles and problems. Ignore them. Jump right in.

My announcement was met with scepticism and some amusement. 'Josh is some joker,' was the general attitude of my family and friends. I'd always done sports. I played rugby at school and I even got into a couple of what can only be called minority-interest games in New Zealand. Gaelic football, for instance, and Aussie Rules. All very well, but the Coast to Coast? The other wedding guests thought I'd had one beer too many.

I was 29 and not fit at that time, either. And working as a plumber didn't afford me a huge amount of exercise. The Coast to Coast included a significant mountain run. The kayaking was through the swift waters of the Waimakariri Gorge. It was a push through some tough country. I couldn't be serious!

Well, I was. And the reaction I got to my announcement firmed up my determination. The others all knew I had been sporty. They probably thought this was a whim and would last as long as the average New Year's resolution. I wanted to prove them wrong. I knew I probably could work up to this event, but would I? I laughed along with them, of course, but the serious training had already started in my mind. A voice quietly spoke in there, 'You think I can't do the Coast to Coast – watch this space.'

The following year, in 2004, that's exactly what I did.

This was a big change for me. I went from doing little, and drinking and smoking besides, to what I then thought was hard training. It was something that would get me away from that unhealthy lifestyle. That was my goal, a sporting challenge. I'd taken on other challenges, of course. Building another room onto my house, for example – now that's a challenge, both physical and emotional! But I wanted to throw my body into an athletic regimen. The Coast to Coast would focus my thoughts into vigorous physical activity. It would awaken the sporting side in me. My days would be all about energy and health.

It would also have other effects that I didn't expect. It would grow a passion for one-on-one competition in me, for example. I realised I loved the sort of sport where you pursue other competitors and pick them off, one at a time. It's not a team you play against, it's individuals, and the contest becomes personal. At the same time, you also test yourself in this event – your willpower, motivation, the ability to press through limitations and endure pain. This was different to team sports where you use your individual talents, sure, but you are always thinking about how you can best serve the unit.

Did I mention that endurance sports are about pain? Pain pervades your entire body – from your toes to your hair follicles. Everything seems to ache, to burn, to grip and tighten. It's punishing but also liberating to realise that you can sustain that effort, that you can go beyond what you thought possible of yourself. This realisation would become fascinating to me, growing over successive events.

And I credit the Coast to Coast for getting me into cycling.

One of the big things for me at the time was giving up cigarettes. I chugged through a pack of tailor-mades a day. Double that after a couple of beers. What's better than a smoke with a bottle of lager? Or after a meal? How good is that relaxed sensation of a full tummy and then a cigarette to give total satisfaction?

I made a couple of half-hearted attempts, and two very serious attempts, to give up. If I didn't have the willpower to give up smoking, how could I make it over a world-class endurance course? Eventually I used a really good pharmaceutical called Zyban. I'd seen an advertisement for this on TV, went to the doctor, then forked out nearly a thousand dollars for a short course, but it worked. It was worth every cent. The cravings completely went and I haven't had a cigarette since.

I know of other people who have tried the same medication, but went straight back to smoking. For me, I think it was a combination of being completely determined to give up, plus having a little help along the way that ended two years of trying to quit, on and off. But I still remember those terrible times of complete self-disappointment when I went back to the habit.

⬡

The Coast to Coast starts with a short run, followed by a road-bike ride of 55 kilometres. Then there's the alpine run over Arthur's Pass, a saddle in the South Island's Southern Alps.

The Alps are a 450-kilometre-long mountain range that run like a spine up the back of the island. The thick bush at the base of these mountains gives way to rock, then summits of the brightest white snow and ice. It's spectacular country – hard, beautiful, unforgiving.

It was still darkish when all the competitors had gathered on Kumara Beach. We'd be running into the breaking dawn. It's a 3-kilometre run to Kumara Junction and the first cycle stage.

Robin Judkins, the bearded and mercurial businessman who founded this event, gave us a 'rark up' through a mega-phone. He's a larger-than-life character, with the energy and enthusiasm of ten men rolled into his small body. He counted down from three then sounded a hand-held air horn. The race had begun.

I scrambled up the stones of the breakwater wall and onto the road, starting out fast, just like I normally do. I run okay, but it's not my favourite thing.

Learning to run again before this event brought home to me just how much my body had lost its spring. I was good at cross-country at school, but that had been 20 years ago. I'd played football since, at a purely social level, but I hadn't concentrated on running and building up distance.

I was living in Ngaio at the time, a leafy, lush suburb on the outskirts of Wellington city. To start off my training,

6

I ran down a few streets then back to my house, perhaps two kilometres, and I felt like my legs had been done over with jackhammers. I was winded and stuffed. How the hell was I going to do 33 kilometres over a mountain pass when a light jog down the road and back made me feel like roadkill? I couldn't bear to think about the other 310 kilometres of exertion on the bike and in the kayak.

At the time, I worked with a guy called Jeff Jewell, an older man who was a good mountain runner. He started me off running again, wrote up a programme that would build up my strength and showed me tracks through the bush.

Every second Sunday, he and his wife would go running with me in the Orongorongo Ranges – which are actually part of the Rimutaka Range on the eastern edge of Wellington Harbour. They are steep, beautiful, bush-covered and rugged hills. The highest peak in this range is Orongorongo at 816 metres.

Running with Jeff got me up to the 10-kilometre mark for mountain runs. Then he had me down at nearby Wilton Park every night. This park on the edge of the city has bush tracks, riverbeds and steep climbs, and it's a good spot to recreate that chill factor that running at altitude inevitably has. Jeff got me doing hill sprints, varying my pace, and building up a picture of how to train and prepare.

I could feel my confidence rising. The next step was to buy a bike. I'd never road-biked competitively before. I picked up a bicycle from a local shop specifically for this event. A Raceline Peleton, it was sleek and light but, as I later found out, too big for me. That's the stuff of a rookie, though.

On my first ride, I started out confidently. I'd ridden mountain bikes up plenty of hills before. But this initial outing completely threw me. I had no idea just how punishing it was to do hill climbs. I'd gone up Makara Hill, behind Karori, a winding climb through hilly sheep farms and lifestyle blocks and down to the coast.

The gears on road bikes are much bigger than mountain bikes, requiring a stronger effort. I came back from that ride destroyed. It should have been easy, I thought. I was surprised at how different road bikes were from mountain bikes. Now I had something else completely new to learn.

I bought some books and studied the training programmes they recommended. It didn't take me long to get used to road biking. I biked everywhere, totting up perhaps 200 kilometres a week, with plenty of hill climbs. That wasn't hard – living in Wellington made hill climbs unavoidable.

With my running and biking training underway, I realised I hadn't even considered the kayak yet. This was something completely alien to me. I was raw and finding my feet – perhaps a strange thing to do at the age of 29.

Twenty-nine? Sure, it's old for getting into a sport. But enduro athletes are just starting to realise their worth at this age. I was stretching my mental toughness, exploring my body's potential, how far it could go, when to push hard and when to hold back. As it happens, starting out later had its advantages. I came to realise this when the first injuries started chewing at my body. Cyclists and multi-sports athletes who have been in the game a long time often have knee and ankle issues, lower back problems, nagging and biting pains from old injuries and accidents. I was starting out injury free.

I achieved my first goal in the Coast to Coast by finishing the running stage and I was ready to move on to the bikes. The first road-bike stage went inland between hills and periodically came alongside the Taramakau, a braided river that runs through a stony river delta. Trout fishing had been a past hobby of mine. I imagined the rainbow trout and salmon beneath the river's glittering surface. It would be a wonderful spot on which to cast a line – but I had other things to do.

The action of water seemed evident everywhere in the landscape. Rain had sculpted the faces of the hills. Riverlets had driven stones down hillsides, grinding out valleys until they became tributaries that fed the tumbling water of the river beside me, eventually rushing to the sea.

This is one of the joys of this sport – finding a harmony with the countryside. Engaging with the land in such a way that you come to understand its physical qualities, along with its sheer, naked beauty.

Cycling gives you a sense of the sweep of the land you're passing through. You move at a pace where you feel its contours, the shifts in the environment around you. It gives you a swift appreciation of its forms, but you don't travel through it so fast that you lose its essential character.

After the bike ride came the alpine run. The rugged terrain tested my strength and stamina. Like the other competitors, I ran up creek beds and big streams, boulder hopping and jumping around the curtains of spray from the waterfalls. It was the heart-thumping, thigh-pumping thousand-metre climb to the top of the pass. And it was cold.

I made multiple river crossings, back and forth, up gullies and sometimes straight up the riverbed. These mountain rivers are largely made from snow melt. They are pretty much as cold as water can be without it being frozen. I ran with a woman runner at this time, helping her with the fords. She knew the route up this part of the course, which was up the Mingha River to Goat Pass. This was great for me – I didn't know the route at all. She ran. I followed.

Over the pass at the top, there are boardwalks to run along. They felt very civilised after the random stacks of rock and paths chiselled out by the attrition of water.

The air is much colder up here. The run takes you through tussock land, the coarse, hardy grasses that grow high up. The angular lines of the Alps are all around. You're as high as some of the glaciers – glistening rivers of ice that shoulder their way through the valleys between peaks. It's uplifting countryside. And with my body pumped full of oxygen and the endorphins set off by the extreme exertion, it was a thrilling experience.

Most people check out the course before they do the race, but I hadn't. I simply didn't have the money to do this. So I was seeing this glorious landscape for the first time. This is a place of heart-stopping beauty. Land that I suspect too few New Zealanders get to see in person.

The 33-kilometre mountain run finishes at a place called Klondyke Corner. The country drops down into the river plateau of the Waimakariri, the river I'd later kayak down. As most people do the race over two days, some 3000 people camped here overnight – support crews who would transport kayaks and other gear, race officials, medics and 800 entrants.

Dianna Bassett, my then partner, and Jeremy Devlin, a mate of mine from Palmy, acted as my assistants for the Coast to Coast, transporting the bike and kayak and setting them up for various stages. What you see in the media coverage of enduro athletes is the hard slog, the starts and finishes, the trophies being handed out. What you don't see are their support crews. A finely tuned, organised and well-balanced crew is essential if an athlete is to perform well.

Jeremy and Dianna had pitched a tent in the campsite. After I'd finished that stage, we fired up a portable gas burner. I'd been eating energy bars and gels, and drinking electrolyte solutions all day. I was starving. That kind of hunger eats a hole in your mind. Your entire middle feels hollowed out. Hot food – even if it is just bacon sandwiches, which is what I had directly after the race – tastes like Christmas dinner. I scoffed those sandwiches down, then later we tucked into pasta for dinner.

This was another lesson I'd pick up with long-distance competitive cycling. You're torching maybe 6000 calories a day. You get down what you can on the move. Often this is just gels with glucose and electrolytes. You just can't get enough sustenance in. Eating well and eating enough becomes an issue – just one of the many tasks the support crew has to get right.

After dinner, we chatted and mingled with others in the race. A holiday atmosphere took over the big campsite. And there was a sense of relief that the first half was over.

At times like this, I come to appreciate my fellow competitors, the grit and training that got them there, the heart and backbone needed to succeed. It's a serious contest, and you take a serious look at those around you to understand their motivation. And you also see glimpses of yourself in their drive and spirit.

An early night was called for, as the next morning would start at 3am. Although the race start wasn't till 7.30, all the gear had to be packed away, and Jeremy and Dianna needed to take the kayak and set it up at the next stage. Before I shimmied into my sleeping bag early that evening, I took in the view above.

The night sky in New Zealand is stunning even in the cities. But away from the city lights it's majestic. The stars crowd the darkness. Their icicle points of light are so clean and bright that they have a piercing quality.

I got into my sleeping bag and thought about the next day. This held the kayaking stage of the race.

I had never kayaked before I decided to do the Coast to Coast. It became part of my build-up to master this sport. The first thing I had to do was buy a kayak. I had checked out a website, Sportzhub, dedicated to second-hand sports equipment, and found an advertisement for an entry-level kayak. It came with a paddle and a lifejacket. Perfect.

One evening after work, I drove around to check it out. Warning: Never buy at night!

I strapped my new purchase to the roof-rack of my plumbing van, drove home, and left it up there overnight. The next morning, I told Dianna about the special purchase. She had a look in the garage at this marvellous new piece of gear, then came back inside and met my proud grin with a quizzical smile.

'It's pink,' she said.

Oh yes, it was. Lipstick pink with purple accents. I felt pink myself whenever I got into it. It was so pink that I was grateful when, on one of the many occasions that I fell out of it, the seat broke. Apparently it was too expensive to get fixed, so I traded it in for another kayak that was in manly shades of red and blue.

To be a part of the Coast to Coast you need to pass a kayaking course that covers grade two rapids. Rapids are graded one to six, with six classified as 'unraftable' and one being the lightest of rapids. Grade two rapids are bumpy enough, but are considered reasonably navigable. I signed up for a grade two training course on the Waikato River.

On the first day of training we practised in short boats in a pool. The instructors tipped us out to make sure that we wouldn't panic. This all went okay.

Then we had a briefing, and the instructor asked if there was anyone present who couldn't swim. No hands went into the air. Until, that is, I sheepishly raised mine.

The instructor's response was uncompromisingly direct: 'By rights, you shouldn't be on this course. We can't stop you from doing it, but if you don't pass the combat swim, you won't get your certificate.' He later explained that if I got into difficulties, there mightn't be anyone around to pull me out. And if there was, they could be risking their life to save mine.

It was gutting to hear. But despite my shameful confession and the instructor's warning, I continued with the course.

In the afternoon, the training took place on a lake. I capsized, the only person on the course to do so, and immediately panicked. I got out from under my boat, bobbing and coughing in the freezing cold water. Everyone had to go home – that ended the day for me and all the other particip-ants because it took so long to get me to shore.

My anxiety was feeding on itself, turning mistake into mishap and apprehension into panic. The next day we actually got on the river. This was the Waikato near its source, Lake Taupo, the lake that would feature so much in my future racing. The Waikato is a big river, wide, with a huge volume of water pumping out of Taupo. Even though we were only kayaking in the flat parts, I found it hard to clamp down on my terror.

We were back on the river on the next weekend of training, spending the first day on the flat areas before progressing the next day to the Reeds Farm rapids. After this part of the course we moved onto the Mohaka River, which can be accessed via the Napier–Taupo highway.

Even after all this training I was still struggling, so I took an extra two days of one-on-one tuition afterwards. This was with a guy called 'Mad Dog', who had apparently paddled the Zambezi River in flood. A big guy with bottle-thick glasses, he wasn't what I expected an ace kayaker to look like. He was blunt and direct. The glasses gave his eyes a sort of faraway, wild look. The name 'Mad Dog' troubled me at first.

But Mad Dog was good for me. The two of us went down the Mohaka. He found a jumping, lively set of rapids called Devil's Elbow, showed me the line and then said, 'Go for it.' He forced me to rely on my own judgement and feel for the white water. After two days, I came out a lot more confident. I felt really good, which was a relief, as the next part of the course would be the grade two testing.

Part of the grade two certificate course was passing what is called a 50-metre 'combat swim'. Back then, an instructor dumped you out of the kayak before rapids, and you had to make it to the shore before you had travelled 50 metres down the river.

When the time came for my combat swim, I kicked out and thrashed around until I finally made it to the bank. I made it to dry ground before the appointed 50-metre mark. It wasn't pretty, but it got me there. If I'd actually had to do legitimate swimming, I wouldn't have passed it. The life-jacket got me through that test.

Racing kayaks are long and narrow – 6 metres in length – built for speed rather than stability. They're straight-line racing boats and are slow to turn. If you capsize, the kayak has flotation bags that keep it on top of the water and a loop of rope on the stern with which to tow it to the bank – a slow and arduous business.

The grade two testing took place on the Whanganui River. The instructor put us through our paces. And everyone did well, including me.

When he finally said, 'Everyone has passed their grade two,' I was jubilant.

We continued down the river. At the next set of rapids, I fell out. I couldn't get to the edge, either, as the river was on the rise. The central current drove forward and dragged me along with it. I had to grab on to the stern of the instructor's kayak and he towed me ashore. It took ages. I asked him if I'd still passed. He just laughed and said I had, and perhaps he shouldn't have said anything.

In reality, passing a grade two rapids course is only the beginning. All it does is establish that you can ride these rapids without killing yourself. From here on in, I needed all the practice I could get.

Shane Ross, a guy in Wellington, organised trips for people getting into multi-sports or who were doing the Coast to Coast. I joined one of the trips where a group of us paddled down the Rangitikei River. Shane was great. He wasn't there to teach, but rather to create training opportunities purely out of his love for the sport. Nonetheless, he was quite knowledgeable and the bunch of athletes I paddled with was quite experienced – their tips and wisdom rubbed off and I learned a lot.

All this paddling, and the fact that I'd joined the Kupe Canoe Club and had worked up my chops, led me to doing my inaugural river race, down the Rangitikei. At the first set of rapids, I flipped over. I felt like I knew this particular rapid as well as the street I drove up every night. I hadn't capsized on it before, but there I was again, looking at the sky wobbling through the waves.

I was determined to get on top of this skill, to nail it. What I absolutely nailed in the next year and a half was capsizing. I fell out of the kayak at every training session. I have the distinction of taking a dip from my kayak in some of New Zealand's major rivers – the Mohaka, the Whanganui, Rangitikei and Waikato rivers. While I was a crap paddler, by this time I was very proficient at capsize safety techniques.

In the kayak courses I did, I learned such things as the best route to follow down the river, and bracing techniques where I would use the paddle to hold the kayak upright to prevent it from capsizing or to halt or slow my movement in the river. I also learned that it's best to scout a river before you kayak down it.

Even with all my experience, when it came to the Coast to Coast, I knew nothing about the Waimakariri River. Or the gorge, extravagantly dubbed New Zealand's Grand Canyon. As I've said, I didn't have the funds to do a recce.

Luckily I met another competitor on the Cook Strait ferry when I was heading down to the South Island from Wellington. He had charts of each of the Waimakariri rapids, including their names and the best lines to follow. He'd done the course before and talked me through the kayaking part of the event. This turned out to be extremely valuable information.

I'm a nervous paddler. And although my competency had grown after a year and a half of training on those wide rivers, I was still being dunked on every excursion.

And I still couldn't swim.

I'd never really thought about my lack of swimming ability too deeply before. I'd done lots of trout fishing in my younger days – and crossed the Rangitikei River waist-deep, sometimes 15 times in one day. Often, at the end of fishing, I'd be crossing the river in the dark. If I'd fallen in . . .

All those times swarmed back into my mind.

Some rivers in New Zealand swallow people whole. You grow up next to them, cross them with bridges, pass them in cars, see them from train windows and from the seats of aeroplanes. You take them for granted, not realising how lethal they can be. But regularly on the news you hear of drownings. Kids jumping off a bridge for fun. Someone tramping and fording a storm-swollen creek. A fall from a bank. An over-turned jetboat. A swimmer snagged by a submerged branch. A kayaker sucked into a swirling hole . . .

The coming day on the Waimakariri was knotting my stomach.

We got up at 3am, as planned, had breakfast and did the packing. After Jeremy and Dianna had left, I got to the start line wearing a throwaway jersey and a plastic rubbish bag with holes for my arms and neck to keep warm.

The first stage on the second day is a 15-kilometre cycle to Mount White Bridge. Then there's an 800-metre run that takes you down to your kayak stationed on the bank of the river.

Also stationed by the bank of the river are race officials who tell you in unnerving tones that this is your last chance to withdraw. Once you hit the Waimakariri Gorge, you can't get out. The sides are high walls of clay and boulders and there are no banks. Once in, there's no turning back. The only way to exit is to paddle through.

I went white. My knuckles went white, too, as I gripped the paddle. If I was nervous before, I was shit-scared now. This sounded serious. That there were a number of race officials there, and that they talked with sober tones like funeral directors, really threw my confidence. This is a kayak leg of 67 kilometres – a good five to six hours on the water. The gorge itself is some 20 kilometres long. But I'd come this far, and been down plenty of rivers – occasionally actually in the kayak – so there was no way I was turning back.

Dianna and Jeremy helped me into the vessel and shoved me out into the flow. I started paddling.

A set of rapids came before the gorge. The familiar bump and hustle of the jostling waves had me cranking my paddle this way and that. Despite my many mishaps, I always enjoyed the white water. There's not enough time to think, just enough to react to your circumstances. By now, I'd developed enough upper body strength to get out of most problems.

I shouted to other paddlers, asking which rapids were coming up, then tried to remember the charts from the ferry ride. Was this a left-hand or right-hand line? This is when 'jump right in' has its drawbacks. Before long, I was back into the rock-and-roll of the tumbling water.

The gorge was a completely different deal. Up ahead, I could see the river narrow as the hills gathered in closer and tighter. The V of the gorge sloped down to the irresistible force of the current at its centre.

The water through the gorge is fast due to the narrowness of the path, but also because the water is dropping down several hundred metres into the rich farmlands of the Canterbury Plains.

When I entered it, I could feel the speed of the river pick up as the water was funnelled in. This was an eerie feeling, a stealthy but intense shift. This powerful concentration of water makes the river seem alive, as if it has its own will and volition. The gorge has bluffs coming down like giant stone pillars, and the water is full of eddies and whirlpools.

Where the water is forced up against the bluffs is the worst part. Or when there's a 90-degree bend, and the water cannons against the rock. If you get sucked into one of these spots, where the water is shoving back on itself, you can get flipped and pinned up against the wall.

There was someone kayaking in front of me, at one point. They were crossing what looked like dead flat water. Then suddenly, they turned turtle, flipped completely upside down. I quickly decided I'd take a different line down that part of the river. Thankfully, the guy handled his recovery well, making for a spot to right his kayak.

There was enough water in the river for me to find 'chicken' routes where I could cut out dangerous corners. It wasn't very efficient racing, but I had no qualms in taking these less-than-courageous paths. I wasn't thinking so much about where I'd be placed at the finish line as about whether I'd still be breathing at the end.

I didn't really notice the exact point at which I came out of the gorge. But I did notice that the countryside had opened out again and the river had braids and the water flow was gentler. Once out of the gorge, there was still another 10 kilometres of paddling to do. I knew how far 10 kilometres was – I could do this.

By this point, the kayak felt so uncomfortable that after every corner I hoped to find the end of the paddling leg. The Waimakariri Bridge signalled this, and at last it came in sight.

There's a warning about the last rapid just before the bridge. Everyone relaxes on this last stretch, thinking that the paddle is over. Then they hit this patch of boiling white water just near the end. Tired paddlers regularly get dunked in these last few metres of the stage. There'd been enough capsizes – I had seen people bailing out their vessels all along the river. I managed to make it through the last patch of white water without tipping out of my kayak. I was stoked.

When I got to the end of the stage, Dianna and Jeremy helped me out of the kayak. After five hours and forty minutes of sitting down paddling, I couldn't feel anything below my waist. Numb. My legs were gone. Once out of the kayak, I stumbled across the rocks and then up a gravel bank to pull on my riding shoes and bike helmet.

The biking was a relief – I knew I could bike 70 kilometres. Actually, I beat my support crew through this final stage. They got stuck in traffic, and I rode past them, waving.

I felt good on the bike ride – I knew I was going to finish, something I hadn't been certain of before I'd got into the kayak. It was a two-and-a-half hour ride to Christchurch. Compared to everything else, biking was my best discipline, and I was passing people. I was amazed at how fresh I felt. People who had been ahead of me were struggling. But here I was, belting along. It felt great.

The ride takes you straight through Christchurch city and out to the coast and Sumner Beach. You ditch your bike, run a bit of a loop on the sand and then you go through a gated channel to the finish line. There was a big crowd on either side of this final run. Under the banner at the end, Robin Judkins waited to congratulate everyone who finished. He loves his race.

I sipped at the beer he'd given me, relieved and exhilarated. Then I realised that I'd paddled the Waimakariri River and gorge without capsizing.

Chapter 2

Cycling away

Each pedal stroke is a pedal away from the past. The odometer rolling over the metres and the pedals turning like the hands of an overheated clock push it further behind me. This energises my legs, grips my mind.

Sometimes it feels like there's been a lot of past to cycle away from – that moment in a courtroom, for instance, when the prospect of prison loomed.

A courtroom isn't the grand structure you see on American TV shows. It's a bland place, like a bare, open-plan office in which no one stays long enough to add personal touches. My future hung in the balance there: a commonplace occurrence for the authorities making the judgement, just another banal day of lives gone wrong.

I was 20 years old, and the run-ins with the law had been growing in frequency since my mid-teenage years. Getting wasted was my week-to-week goal. Sport no longer had a place in my life. That had departed when my parents separated.

I was 30 when they eventually broke up. But this had been brewing for some time. I trace it back to when Dad left the army. This, to me, is when things started to go bad for them.

⚶

My father had been a lance corporal in the Engineer Corps – the bridge builders, the road and airfield makers who support an active force. Us kids would tag along with him on Saturdays when he went to work at Linton Military Camp, just outside of Palmerston North. It was such a cool place for a kid to hang out.

I'd watch him play rugby for the army team at the camp. His side of the family was really sporty. All my cousins played rugby. I was a scrawny little kid, but reasonably good at most codes. I played various sports – softball, cricket, tennis, even hockey. I was also a strong cross-country runner and fast over short distances. In sprints, I always came first or second. For a while, I settled on soccer as my main sport.

And Dad was always there with Mum on Saturday when I played for the Cloverlea School team. My grandparents would come from Otaki to watch me play, too. Dad teased me that soccer was a sissy game, but in my first season he agreed to pay me a dollar for every goal I scored. He didn't count on me scoring 45 times that year! It was an offer he didn't repeat. I usually played as a winger, so the incentive was very effective. It wasn't so good for my brother, Kane – he was a defender. In the end, to be fair, I had to split my money with him.

I got up to all the usual mischief as a kid. I remember once sneaking biscuits into bed. I hid under the covers so that Kane wouldn't find out as I munched them. It's one of those silly, really-easy-to-detect 'crimes', and I got caught. Dad came into my room in the morning and was going to give me the strap. I pretended to be asleep, and he didn't want to wake me up as he'd also wake Kane and Natasha, so I managed to dodge that hiding.

Dad left the army after he was medically downgraded because of a knee injury. In the army in those days you still had to pass physicals. Medical downgrading meant he couldn't advance any further than his current rank. It must have been quite a blow for someone who was so physically active. The end result would have been him taking a desk job, which wouldn't have been that appealing to him. He was like a lot of men back then. He'd fix his own car and make sure everything was spick and span around the property, always doing something.

We lived in Cloverlea, a new subdivision back then. It had houses made with HardiePlank, those broad weatherboards, and aluminium frames on the windows, on typical flat, green Palmerston North sections. The area was young, full of new families. There were lots of kids in our street and we all went to the Cloverlea Primary School – it was sociable and fun.

When Dad stepped out of the army, he walked into a city where he didn't know anyone. His working life in Palmerston North had all been about the army. He just went from job to job. He couldn't settle into any of them. I was a kid at the time and didn't understand, but I knew that something was not right.

Mum married Dad when she was 16, and had me when she was 18. She'd had no time on her own. It was her 28th birthday that year. A teenager when she married, a woman now.

They split up. There weren't any arguments or anything like that. After a while, they tried getting back together, but it didn't work out. Dad hung around Palmy for a while, then shifted to his home town, Otaki, and back to his extended family. I didn't see much of him after that. He wasn't the best at keeping in contact and he forgot birthdays, especially Kane and Natasha's.

I get a lot of my traits from my mother. A stubborn, determined person, she's got a really strong work ethic. She wasn't the sort to go on the Domestic Purposes Benefit, the New Zealand governmental support for solo parents. Instead she worked two jobs, sometimes three, to bring up us kids. We had no car for three years. I remember going on a school camp and walking halfway across Palmy with these heavy packs to get to college.

We moved from Cloverlea to a rental in Highbury. There were scary moments for Mum in this new life. In this particular property, we got robbed a month before Christmas. All the presents got stolen from Mum's bedroom, where she'd been hiding them from us. She was really shaken. I was at

Dad's place for the night and had to come home to stay with her. I don't know how much comfort and security a skinny little 12-year-old could offer her, but I was the oldest male in the household.

Because Mum worked so much – and Dad had moved away – neither of them were there to watch me play soccer on Saturdays any more. I began to drift away from sports. Some essential purpose had fallen out of my effort on the field. My heart wasn't in it.

We moved from the rental in Highbury to a state house in the same suburb. It was a semi-detached dwelling with a wall dividing us from the house next door. You could hear the people thumping around through this wall – and I guess they could hear us. The worst thing about this was hearing the man next door getting violent. He would beat up his wife and we heard it all. I hated this sickening sound, the brutality coming muffled through the wall.

Mum called the cops on him once. Then he threatened her. Looking back, this was an oppressive environment with few exits – a place full of a bleak poverty and despair.

My brother and I were picked on, too. More than once we were chased home after school by glue-sniffers. On one occasion, my brother had a 'glue bag' thrown in his face and he got paint in his eyes. He had to be carted off to hospital to have his eyes rinsed out.

They also stole our bikes and washing off the line. A creek ran down the back of our row of houses. A low wire fence divided our backyard from a path that ran above it. The sniffers hung out underneath a bridge the creek passed beneath, so it was easy for them to just hop over the fence and help themselves to our stuff.

We were too small to fight these guys outright, but I developed a sneaky strategy. Kane and I stationed ourselves at either side of the bridge, and from a distant vantage point, we biffed stones at them. Big ones. They couldn't avoid the crossfire, and we had the advantage both of being above them and of not having solvent flowing through our veins . . .

The organisation and rhythm of life changed without Dad. I used to help out by making the dinner. Mum wasn't there to make tea herself. She would get stuff prepared and I would cook it. I had to put it on at the right time so that it was ready for when Mum came home, and then Natasha and Kane and I could have it with her.

In the morning I would do a paper run, and after school I'd go to a joinery shop to sweep floors. For the paper run, I'd get up at five in the morning. There were a couple of dogs I'd need to negotiate during the run – they were both labradors. One, I remember, was in Monrad Street. I'd sneak up quietly to the house where it lived at about 5.30 in the morning. I knew that when it chased me, it would only go as far as the intersection, then it would stop. So as long as I made that intersection, I was all right. It was a bit of work, pedalling flat out with the bike loaded up with newspapers. I ended up dropping the paper run – the joinery shop paid more.

I always biked. This was especially good in Palmy because it's so flat. One of my favourite things to do was to get fence palings and make little ramps. I'd line up the younger kids in front of the ramp on the road and see how many I could jump over. I always cleared them. I don't know whether that was my athletic prowess, or the survival instinct of those kids ensuring that they wouldn't go longer than I could clear.

It must have been around the time Mum and Dad split up that I joined the St John Ambulance cadets – this was a big part of my life for a while. Someone came to our school and gave a talk about it. I thought it sounded interesting and useful and checked it out.

My friend Dion and I joined at the same time. We both went to Monrad Intermediate. Dion was my main rival on the sports field. In sprints, it would be me and him vying for first and second place at the finish line. I got the advantage on him after he broke his ankle – he couldn't quite muster the pace after it had healed. Dion joined the St John cadets so he could get out of doing the dishes after dinner for a night.

It was a bit like Boy Scouts, in that when you achieved a certain level of proficiency in various things you earned badges. We practised nursing care and first aid up to level two. And we got involved in Zambuck duty at the stock cars and at rugby matches as well as other sporting events, giving first aid when needed. The name 'Zambuck', I later learned, came from a trade name for an ointment that had a black-and-white tube – the St John Ambulance uniform is black and white.

At the stock cars, we'd stand out in the middle of the oval at Rainbow Stadium. When crashes happened, once the race officials had cleared it and said it was safe, we'd make sure no one was injured. I remember absolutely freezing out on

Colquhoun Park, watching the rugby, waiting for something to happen. No one liked rugby duty. When somebody went down, us Zambucks would go on with the 'magic ice water', slosh a bit on and then the injured player would usually be all right. We were allowed to pull players off the field for concussion injuries. We had to make sure they got to hospital. The refs were quite good, but you used to get a bit of abuse from the players. We were just kids, and we were going out there saying that they couldn't play on. We did have one adult supervising us as well.

We went to St John Ambulance competitions all around the country – and won quite a few. We'd work in teams on mocked-up accident scenes, with people with made-up injuries and fake blood who would act out the part. We learned marching drill at the cadets and won competitions for that too.

In 1986, there was a big nurses' strike around the country and we ended up working in hospital wards. I was about 13 at the time and was in a terminal illness ward full of old people in Palmerston North Hospital. We were doing mundane duties, changing bedpans, doing bed baths for all these old people. It was quite an eye-opener. The old folks thought it was great. And sometimes we would sit and talk to them for a while.

Just recently, I was doing some work on the Kapiti Coast and I came across an accident – a young boy had been knocked off his motorbike. All these people were standing around this guy who was crawling along the road in complete shock. No one was helping him. I pulled up because I had a first aid kit in the van and I thought I might be able to help.

I got him to stop moving. He was on his hands and knees. He said that there was something wrong with his hip. So I felt his hip, then I saw all this blood running down the grass. I said to the guy, 'Mate, I've got to move you, you're bleeding.' I thought the blood was coming from his abdomen so I put gloves on and rolled him over. I looked down at his leg, and his kneecap was completely gone.

Then I got these girls to stop traffic, and asked if someone had called an ambulance yet. There was just panic. Another car pulled up and a lady got out and said, 'I'm a nurse, can I help?' I said, 'Yeah, you sure can.' I took care of the knee while she talked to him.

Eventually he was choppered to Wellington Hospital. I think he had lost a lot of blood. I got back into the van, thinking that was an intense five minutes – or however long it had taken, it was kind of hard to tell.

But all that stuff from St John came straight back to me without me even thinking about it. I'd done so much of it, I suppose, that it's permanently etched into my brain. I knew I shouldn't move him because I didn't know what his injuries were. I could feel his hips, they didn't feel smashed up or anything. And if he had crawled that far, he obviously didn't have a broken back. That's a lot of movements. He was crawling along without a kneecap, but he was in such shock he had no idea.

🚲

I met Marie Kapluggin at the cadets. Being rather bossy, she became our team leader. I guess you'd describe her as odd.

She was a couple of years younger than me, a little girl who always walked around with a handbag like an adult. She was different, but I accepted her for who she was. We ended up being very good friends. That's carried on right through life.

Marie took a straighter path than me – you don't get much straighter than Marie. But she was always there for me through all the bad years. She knew what was happening with me but she didn't lecture me. If someone told me not to do something, I was probably going to do it anyway, so there was no point in just going on at me. But actually being there when I did fall, that was probably more helpful.

She eventually moved to Hawke's Bay. After that, we saw each other now and again, at twenty-firsts and things like that. But we were always in contact. We used to write to each other – back when you still wrote letters to people.

I did St John cadets until I got kicked out of Mum's place and went to live with Dad. Just before then, I was moving away from that group of St John people and getting in with another crowd.

The best part of my childhood was when I stayed with my grandparents, on my mother's side. My grandfather is someone I aspire to be like. He managed farms and on school holidays I would help him out. He worked on a big Tegel poultry farm when I was at primary school, and a beef farm when I was in my teenage years. On the poultry farm, I'd feed the chickens as they wandered around in these big sheds, and help out in the egg room where the eggs were cleaned and graded.

He took me out deer hunting. I didn't care what my friends were doing during the holidays – I'd hang out at my grandparents' place. My grandfather ended up being my father figure. But I still missed my dad.

I didn't really speak to my grandfather on my father's side, not until I was 16, just before he died. A very quiet man, he couldn't relate to kids. We sat down to have a game of chess. And that was the only time we had a conversation. He fought the Japanese during World War II and had carried one of his dead mates off the battlefield. I remember him sitting in his La-Z-Boy chair, drinking home brew, listening to classical music and taking care of his pet birds.

My nana on that side was a real hard case, the total opposite of my grandfather. She used to knit, eat lollies and watch Chuck Norris movies. In the last year and a half before she died, I spent quite a bit of time with her. She had all the cool stories about early Courtenay Place and going out dancing in Wellington. She showed me photos of Grandad with his shirt unbuttoned and a gold chain hanging down. The women were all wearing low-cut tops. They were quite trendy back then.

I was close to my great-grandfather, too. The family used to call him 'Mr Haka'. There's a really cool photo that sums him up 100 per cent. He's a little man and he's got these old pants on, cut off at the bottom because he's so short, and tied up with a piece of rope. He's standing on this hill with one of those old wire strainers for fences and he's pulling that tight, his forearms are bulging. He was renowned for being an exceptionally hard worker.

☙

When I left school I wanted to be a builder, but there was just no work. You couldn't get that sort of work anywhere. I was 17. The next year I spent bumming around, pretty much doing nothing. Getting into trouble.

Mum met her current partner, Brian, when we were living in Highbury. He broke up with his wife and then moved into our house. The poor bugger walked into a disaster zone. The second night after he moved in, the police dropped me off at home drunk. My brother and sister were crying upstairs. He must've wondered what the hell he'd gotten into.

We didn't get along. I wouldn't have gotten along with him if he'd been a rock star or a saint. I wasn't getting along with anyone, particularly someone in my house who might try to get me in line. There was also a cultural gap between us. He was sort of an old-fashioned Pom – at least that's how I saw him then. He drove a brown Rover with tan leather seats – reason enough to dislike anybody. He used to work on the railways. When he came to live with us, he was the manager of a cleaning company. We get along fine now. Things improved between us after I left home. Or rather, when Brian kicked me out. I don't blame him – I was out of control.

This seemed to happen suddenly, but my antics must have been wearing Brian and Mum down for some time. It was on Natasha's birthday that everything came to a head. The night before, I had been partying and was a total wreck and still smashed on something. A bunch of family members were coming around for Natasha's birthday and Mum yelled at me to get up the stairs to have a shower. My Aunty Pam was already there, and apparently she was terrified of me while I was in this wasted condition.

I went upstairs. All I remember is falling down and grabbing hold of the shower rail and the whole thing came crashing down. My grandfather ran in, picked me up and chucked me into my room. That was the finish of me living at Mum's.

I stayed with my grandparents that night, and the next day I was living with my father. He made it clear that I needed to be doing something, which meant going back to school. I'd already been out of college for a year by then. I duly went back, but it was a mistake. Teachers were always telling me what to do, and I'd say, 'Whatever.'

While I was staying at Dad's, my grandfather – his dad – passed away. And Mr Haka, my great-grandfather on Mum's side, also died. He was like a rock in our family.

I stopped going to school. I just hung around town. Eventually Dad found out. He said, 'Right, you've got to get a job.' I applied for a couple of jobs and got one with a transport company doing furniture removals. That lasted for a couple of years.

For driving the truck and humping furniture around, up and down hills, with Wellington steps and bad access-ways, I earned the princely sum of $150 a week.

My job in the morning was to fill up the removal truck with unleaded petrol. On one occasion, by the time we'd driven from Paraparaumu to Khandallah, blue smoke was pouring out of the back of the truck. The boss was worried, wondering out loud, 'What's wrong with my truck?'

We took it to a garage, but the guy there didn't know what was wrong, so he said to drive it back to our regular mechanic in Paraparaumu. The boss sent me home for the day. That was Monday. He gave me a call at home on Wednesday. I was still living at my father's place. Dad came to me and said, 'Your boss is on the phone and he doesn't sound too happy.' My boss said, 'I'm coming around to pick you up – we're going to the mechanic's.'

We went there and the mechanic poured two different liquids on the ground. He said, 'Do you know the difference between petrol and diesel?' As soon as he said that, I felt sick. The mechanic held a match to these. The petrol flamed and the diesel did nothing. He went on, 'One lights and one doesn't.'

The boss made me work Saturdays for nothing for the next six months. I hauled all that furniture, those refrigerators and lounge suites for six days a week and earned $150 dollars for it.

Dad, by this time, had a new partner. They moved from Paraparaumu, so I went flatting. I ended up having enough of the furniture moving business. A mate and I decided to shift to Napier. Why Napier? I have no idea. Jump right in! It was a totally random move.

Neither of us had jobs, so we were both on the unemployment benefit. We did nothing – just sat around all day and progressively fell in with the wrong people.

This resulted in us having to leave Napier in a hell of a hurry – we had a run-in with one of the local gangs. We were only 17 or 18, and a friend's mother was going out with a gang member.

One night – actually, about two in the morning – we came back from a party, and our friend was sitting on the porch, so we said, 'Come in.' He came inside and left the door open, and the next thing these big guys came bowling in. They said, 'We're taking your stuff.' I told them where they could stick that notion. Then smack! I was flat on my back on the floor.

I ran outside and knocked on the neighbour's door. They rang the police on me.

Meanwhile, the gang members had taken half of our stuff. I was quite naïve, and when the police arrived, I told them where this gang was holed up.

We went around there, and walked through the house with the cops, pointing out which things were ours. All these gang members were sitting around saying under their breath, 'You're dead.'

Once we got back to the flat, it dawned on me what I'd done. We packed up our stuff that night and I rang up Mum and said, 'Have you got a trailer? We need to get out of here.'

But we couldn't leave straight away. We had to close down the flat and sort out the power before we moved back to Palmy. It was a very nervous week, and we were sneaking around the streets of Napier very quietly.

I had a few bad years. I was doing nothing with my life, working under the table doing demolition. Looking back, it seems just about right. I imagined being a builder when I left school, but I was doing the opposite. Smashing things apart, breaking them down. Things were getting worse and worse, both with the crowd I was hanging with and my living situation. Then someone organised some work for me with a plumber called Lance Davis.

I laboured with him for a couple of years. After we worked with another company for a couple of days, they said to Lance, 'If you don't give Josh an apprenticeship, we'll give him one.' So he offered me an apprenticeship. I would have sooner gone with Lance – we got on really well.

Then I hit the wall.

I had been in trouble with the law a few times – wilful damage, marijuana possession, theft, drunk and disorderly. The cops had picked me up staggering around the streets too many times. I ended up in court and facing the possibility of being imprisoned. My life and liberty were in someone else's hands. I stood there like a dummy and could see the future unravelling in front of me.

But I had just been offered this apprenticeship, so I was given a last chance. That apprenticeship kept me out of the slammer.

Lance really gave me a break. None of my other friends had jobs. I had to keep out of trouble. That thought saw me gradually move away from that aimless group, and the flat I lived in. I moved out one night. I didn't tell anyone, I just needed to get out. Needles had started to appear in that flat. They were shooting up and I wasn't going to take things that far. So I left.

I met Dianna Bassett around this time. We flatted together for a little while, then the flat disbanded. We met again at a party, and I walked her home. I think I just kept hanging around and annoying her until she gave in and became my girlfriend. She was the first proper girlfriend I'd had since school – it was a serious relationship.

I started to have a normal life after that. I had a lot of friends who saw me through a lot of that. People like Marie Kapluggin. And my mum never saw the bad in me.

I worked hard. I'd spend weeks and weeks digging drains. I'd never complain. I never showed up late. I'd walk from one side of Palmy to the other to get to work. And I'd walk home. I never asked for a ride or anything. I was working pretty hard, breaking up concrete. It was two years of doing shitty work, and slowly learning how to do plumbing.

My boss would sometimes get someone to help me dig these long drains. For some reason he thought big guys would be better at it. These burly fellas would show up and by lunchtime they'd be gone. I'd say to him, 'You need to get someone skinny and hungry.'

Every pedal stroke is a pedal away from the past. If I go hard for long enough, it will be way back behind me.

Some riders, when they do a hill climb, put their heads down, concentrate on their cadence, the rhythm stroke of riding. That way, their concentration is not on the hill, how far they have to climb, the summit before them. I don't. I look up, intent on the top. That's where I'm going. Up there. Every pedal stroke takes me there.

Chapter 3

From Taupo to Paris

The Coast to Coast got me in the saddle and gave me a feel for road-bike racing. This would eventually attract me to races around Lake Taupo, and later, the famous Paris–Brest–Paris (PBP) brevet in bike-mad France – an enthralling event, full of Gallic passion and hospitality.

A brevet is not strictly speaking a race, it's a 'friendly'. Yeah, right.

But before I got hooked on road-bike racing, I fooled around with mountain bike competitions. I'd been riding mountain bikes for years and loved cranking around the bush and mountain-bike tracks around Palmerston North. A friend of mine, Jerry, an Irish guy who had introduced me to Gaelic football, also introduced me to mountain biking.

He lent me his bike so I could go for a ride with a friend of his. I managed to beat this guy on a ride up a hill and sat at the top having a cigarette while I waited for him to catch up. Then I started riding with Jerry quite regularly. Most days after work, we'd hoon around all over the place.

Once I biked down to Otaki from Palmerston North with a mate of mine, Karl. Not only did we carry our backpacks, we also had spare tyres, and a cask of wine – quite a load. We camped up Otaki Gorge and biked back on Sunday.

I also entered a mountain-bike race in Palmerston North. My bike shorts consisted of a pair of cut-off black jeans, and I wore my plumber's raincoat to keep off the wet because it was hosing down on the day of the race. I was biking up Scotts Road and some guy felt sorry for me and picked me up at the bottom. The race was cancelled but I did the course anyway.

Almost directly after the Coast to Coast, I did the 12-hour Moonride, a mountain-bike race up in Rotorua over an 8-kilometre circuit. It started at 10 in the morning and finished at 10 at night, and the winner was the rider who completed the most laps.

I hadn't done anything like it before. I just rocked up and didn't realise how I was going to feel afterward. At that stage, it was the longest single event I'd done. The Coast to Coast was split over two days, with each day taking less than 12 hours. How difficult could the Moonride be after the mountain run and the wild ride down the Waimakariri River?

I had a 'hard-tail' mountain bike – it had no suspension on the back – with just a little front suspension. It was made of aluminium, very stiff and very jarring. But I wasn't too concerned. The circuit was a smooth, plush ride with a sweet flow to it and nicely bevelled edges when you swung into the corners. Set in Whakarewarewa Forest, it was a gorgeous track with mature redwood trees, ferns and big punga fronds hanging down. It was a stunning place, fresh and green.

I pumped around the track, going flat-out with this 'hard tail'. Despite the smooth track, I felt every vibration. This was fine at first. But as all the riders churned up the circuit, ruts deepened and roots of trees became exposed. And as the night set in and the air cooled, moisture condensed on these roots, making them slippery.

After a while, I felt every rut and gnarled protuberance, the vibrations shuddering up my arms, my back, my butt. Square wheels would have been more comfortable. I banged along, refusing to quit – that was just not my plan, that's never my plan.

As the ride hammered on, I stopped noticing how lovely the setting was. It felt like I had bolts rattling around in my head. Each time I slammed into another dip, my whole body shook.

I didn't have a support crew with me for this race – I was there alone. I thought that I'd just camp at the venue afterward. But I didn't count on how bad I was going to feel at the finish. I was absolutely buggered and sore in every place imaginable. After 12 hours sitting on a mountain bike with my body being used like a huge shock absorber, just getting

43

off the bike, loading up the car and driving felt like trying to wade through a sea of porridge.

I hadn't really looked this race up – I'm not sure if I would have been any better prepared if I had. That's the way I've always done things. Go for it. It'll be okay.

Luckily I found a hotel in Rotorua that I could get into at 11 at night. The next day, during the five-hour drive home to Wellington by myself, I struggled to stay awake, the exhaustion gnawing at the inside of my head. This was no iron-man driving, I was a jelly-man. Then on the Himitangi 'straights', those long stretches of straight highway through the Manawatu, I got a flat tyre. It may as well have been a zombie changing the wheel. It was an epic effort to get home. And I was shattered for days afterwards.

I came 11th out of 50-odd riders in that race. Not a bad result for an inexperienced hack. At the time, it felt like a major achievement just getting through that ride. I look back now and think that it was only 12 hours . . .

I did mountain-bike racing off and on for the next few years with mixed results. I came third in the 2006 Moonride, which I thought was pretty good. But my focus was switching to road-bike contests. The Coast to Coast had given me a taste – I wanted more.

Around 26,500 years ago, a massive volcanic eruption ripped a hole in the centre of New Zealand's North Island, and caused hundreds of square kilometres of surrounding land to collapse. Many more eruptions followed, with another huge blast around 1800 years ago. The resulting crater filled with water to form Lake Taupo. Volcanic ridges became reefs in the lake and a series of hills around its perimeter. It's considered a dormant rather than an extinct volcano.

The hilly profile around the lake's perimeter comprises part of the 160-kilometre Cycle Challenge course. It takes three-and-a-bit laps to make up a 500-kilometre course. This would be my first road-bike endurance race, the 2005 Taupo Super Enduro.

Taupo is a tough and memorable course. The International Cycling Union has named it one of the best rides in the world. Of the seven international events in the union's prestigious Golden Bike race series, five are in Europe, one is in South Africa, and the other one is here, in the centre of the North Island.

I thought I'd done a lot of training going into it, but I was green. I still had no idea, really. Although, at least this time I had a support crew – Dianna Bassett, her sister, Christine, and her dad, Des.

My local bike shop in Johnsonville, J'ville Cycles, gave me a lot of assistance. Blair, a guy who worked there, was into endurance cycling. He used to do the two-lap Taupo race, and he gave me a lot of help, advising me on good lightweight wheels that weren't too expensive. We settled on American Classic 350s. As I upgraded my Raceline, it became lighter – and every few grams you remove means the less weight you haul around long distances. Each gram seems to grow heavier with each kilometre you cycle and with each kilojoule of energy you push out of your body. The lighter the bike, the better.

With the lake being 160 kilometres around and the race being made up of three laps, an extra 20 kilometres was needed to make up the 500. This meant the start was 20 kilometres out of Taupo, virtually at the top of a place called Hatepe Hill, a climb that many riders find daunting.

The competitors congregated in a carpark where several logging trucks were parked. I looked around at the other riders. There was one guy driving a gleaming Land Rover Discovery. He had a trailer decked with the flashest bikes. This was Steve Sharpe – a builder from Queenstown, sharp by name and sharp in his ability. My own modest gear felt shabby and mundane. The pre-race anxiety was eating a hole in my middle. Let's get on with it!

When we assembled at the start line, Keith Crate, the main organiser, was walking around having a word with the riders. Then he looked at me and said, 'Have you done Taupo before?' And I said, 'Nah.'

I hadn't even done one lap in training. I hadn't biked the lake at all, and didn't know anything about the course.

Keith said, 'Don't you think you should've, perhaps, done a lap first to see what it was like?' It seemed to me that I was doing all right with endurance sports and, despite the pre-race nerves, I had a cocky rejoinder: 'You let me worry about my race and you worry about *organising* the race.'

Then we did a parade for the first 20 kilometres, all cruising along at the same speed, so it wasn't really racing. I wanted to get on with the competition, and this public spectacle, although probably a great promotion for the event, felt like a waste of time. My legs wanted to drive into action.

After Taupo township, we'd be into it. Just outside of Taupo, I needed to take a pee. I stopped and all the rest of the riders just left me there! I was astonished. I assumed everyone would wait and we would do the first lap together, but they just shot off. The first guy I caught up with when I started riding again was an older guy nicknamed 'Crunchy'. I was quite miffed that everyone had taken off, but he explained to me that in enduro races, everyone bikes at their own pace. Then I understood. I left him and started biking past everybody.

There is no doubt that the circuit is demanding. There are no long climbs – they're all short, but they're constant. Just outside of Taupo, I hit the first hill. This, I would discover, is where all the sorting out happens for the enduro racers. In subsequent Taupo races, this is where I would first attack. By the time I'd get to the top of the hill I'd be in the leading bunch and then I'd know who my real rivals would be for the rest of the race.

After this hill is a turn that leads to the western side of the lake. From here, there's a gentle climb that rises to the highest point in the race. This is the toughest part in the race for me. At the end of each lap, I know that the first hill is coming and then that climb, which more often than not is into a headwind. It's a gradual climb, but you can feel your body working the whole time. If I wasn't going very well, this is where things would become tough for me. On the other hand, if my energy was up, I could really make other competitors hurt badly through this section.

Then there is a turn that goes to the 'back' of the lake, the narrow road that snakes past farmland to Kuratau. The first part of the road is rolling country. Closer to Kuratau is a series of climbs – short, sharp, unrelenting. The route has 1650 metres of climbing in total – now multiply this by three for the 500-kilometre race. And eight times for the 1280-kilometre race. As you move on, it starts taking it out of you.

But this can also be one of the most exhilarating sections of the race. On a clear day, you get this perfect view of Mount Ruapehu. Beyond the farmland, its snow-covered cone rises out of the mist. Sometimes you see 'smoke' coming from its bubbling crater lake. It's an amazing sight that lifts your heart as you power toward it. The more exhausted you become, the more impressive this mighty volcano seems.

⬡

Despite what people say, I find most truckies are pretty good around cyclists. On the other hand, I've gotten used to trucks careering past. If you cycle for long enough, you're bound to have 'moments' with all sorts of vehicles.

I had my fair share of logging trucks pass me on that first Taupo Super Enduro. The race follow vehicle sticking out behind the pack provides a measure of protection. This vehicle has hazard lights on it and a big sign saying that a cycle race is in progress. But there are still risks.

On the first lap, I was coming around the eastern side of the lake, on the thin, twisting road towards Taupo township. It's an irony that in the 160-kilometre course around Lake Taupo, you only see this enormous body of fresh water for about 30 kilometres of it. During the day, this main thoroughfare into the town gets busier.

Because there's one sharp bend after another, my support vehicle had pulled back to give me room. A logging truck overtook it and got in between us. Then on yet another corner that turned back on itself, the truck overtook me. After it blew past in a gust of diesel, no one from the support vehicle could see me. It was obvious that it had cut out all of my road space. Des thought I'd been sideswiped into the lake.

They stopped and found me still on my bike. The truck had forced me off the road and over the gravel edge and right up to the barrier fence on the side. I wasn't hurt – or too bothered. Crap happens. It's happened before and it will happen again. After Des had checked me out, I got back on my bike and back into the race.

It took me 19 hours 40 minutes to finish. It was quite a fast time at that point in the history of the 500-kilometre Enduro, but the weather was good that year – it had been cold around the back of the lake, but not too bad.

At one point in the race I was coming second, but eventually I got passed by another rider on the third lap. I got pipped by two guys from Queenstown and finished third – Steve Sharpe, the rider with the impressive four-wheel drive and the even more impressive bikes, won the race.

I was pretty sore after that, but rapt because that was my first really big race – 500 kilometres is long by anyone's standards. I thought that I'd done pretty well, too, and knew then that I would go back and do it again. I liked this style of racing.

In 2006 I did a 230-kilometre race, the Tour de Manawatu, and that's when I first heard about the Paris–Brest–Paris (PBP). It's also where I met Colin Anderson – this guy is the 'Sir Ed' of enduro cycling in New Zealand. He is an absolute legend. His attitude is 'Let's get on and get this done'. That's Colin. I eventually rode with him a lot and remember quite a few times just trying to hang on to his wheel, to stay alive. He's got the record for the most laps around Taupo, the record for cycling the length of New Zealand, records all over the place. He's a straight-talking man, who was in his fifties back then.

I cycled with him for quite a while during the Tour de Manawatu, and he filled me in on the PBP. Colin and a guy called Douglas Mabey both talked about it. I thought that it sounded pretty good. The PBP was only held every four years and it was coming up the next year, in 2007.

I also learned that the Tour de Manawatu had been recognised as a qualifier for the PBP, so I was on the road to it already . . . and several of the riders in this race were out to qualify. Then the next Taupo Enduro race was made a PBP qualifier as well.

I didn't know how to use a computer in those days, so Dianna looked up the race to find out more. The Paris–Brest–Paris is a 1200-kilometre race from France's inland capital to Brest on the north-western coast of Brittany, then back to Paris again. A couple of things made me hesitate over the race: Could I afford it? And could I actually bike that far?

To qualify for the PBP, you had to do 200, 300, 400 and 600 kilometre events. These had to be finished within specified times – 14, 20, 28 and 40 hours respectively. This included all rest time and stops, which meant an average speed of around 15 kilometres per hour to qualify. This seemed reasonably easy.

Leading up to the next Taupo race – the Maxi Enduro – I was just doing races that were official qualifying events for the PBP. I did heaps of them. Even if I didn't need to do them I did, just for training.

The 2006 Taupo Cycle Challenge Super Enduro was a straight four-lap, 640-kilometre race around the lake. This was the longest qualifying distance I needed to be eligible for the PBP.

That was my biggest race up until then. The distances were building up.

In this race, I ended up at the front with Colin Anderson and Steve Sharpe. We were all going about the same speed. We stuck together on the first lap. On the second lap, the weather turned bad – it was absolutely pouring with freezing rain. I've never felt so cold on a bike. At that point, the three of us decided we'd stay together.

It was a lesson on how cold it can get when you're a little bit damp, and the wind's coming onto you. Even though it was late spring, there was snow on the mountains and the wind coming off them carried a significant wind chill factor. At one point the temperature was below zero.

I put on every piece of clothing I could get from my follow vehicle to keep warm and just tried to hang on until the truck stop at Turangi. A hamburger and chips beckoned, and the prospect of eating something hot kept me going.

We stuck together to battle against the wind and the cold, for the company and the motivation. Just as it was turning dark, the rain came down harder than ever, a Niagara of icy water. For the next couple of laps it was really bad – the deluge bashing a bitter chill into us.

Steve Sharpe had a really bad period. Colin and I drafted him for a bit. This is when a rider follows right behind your slipstream, or 'draft', which creates a suction effect. They can effectively reduce their effort by up to 30 per cent while doing the same speed as you. For the second and third laps he wasn't feeling good. The last lap around I was feeling like mud, the rain knocking the heart out of me. Colin stopped for a rest, and Steve drafted me for this lap. We were getting close to Turangi, and I was feeling close to being uncon-scious. Steve just took off at this point. And I thought, 'I helped you out for all that time – fantastic!' But when I got to the truck stop, he was waiting for me. He told me to hurry up, that we had to keep on going. As soon as I had something to eat, I felt a lot better.

We both got to the main street of Taupo together and we were up for second and third. Steve said, 'How are we going to decide this?' I said, 'I dunno.' Then Steve said, 'We're going to have a sprint, aren't we?'

The crowd at Taupo were amused at two enduros up off their saddles and pumping up a sprint. There were a couple of cheers and lots of raucous laughter and hands clapping. Steve had a little more gas in the tank than me and he eventually took second. He did, however, shout the beer at the finish line.

One rider came in before us – that was Peter Cole. He was the guy I would end up racing for the next few years for first place.

Peter was quite a rival. In February 2007, we were both riding in a 400-kilometre race, which was another qualifier for the PBP. This race was a 400-kilometre loop that did one circuit of Lake Taupo, then went out to Reporoa and back. There was me, Colin Anderson and Peter Cole. Peter and Colin started attacking on the big hill over to Taumarunui. I thought, what the heck is going on? This was an incredibly hot, cloudless day, the sun was blindingly bright and heat streamed up in transparent waves from the bitumen road.

Pete got ahead of the two of us. He disappeared over the top of the hill and Colin and I just faded in the heat. We didn't see Pete again until the finish line. He was a good rider, and someone I thought I was going to be chasing forever. He didn't go to the PBP, however, because of family commitments.

I didn't have a cycling coach back then, but my personal trainer at the gym, Brad Quinn, was pretty good. He worked on my core strength, building up this essential element of my fitness. And he made up a bit of a programme for me. On a Tuesday night after 4pm, I'd go down Ngaio Gorge and up Ngauranga Gorge and then back down Ngauranga and up Ngaio to make up one circuit. I had to do that 12 times. The Ngauranga Gorge is a curving 2-kilometre climb with a grunty 8 per cent gradient. Around 65,000 cars pass through the gorge each day. At evening rush hour, the cars going up the multiple lanes of the gorge moved like a big metal river. The ride down Ngauranga was less congested, but still busy. The Ngaio Gorge was shorter and narrower – just a single lane each way – and less steep at 5.7 per cent gradient. This was a faster and fresher climb, as it wound up through abundant bush. I started out in daylight, at rush hour, then the cars would thin and night would fall.

I'd still be out there until 11 o'clock doing these hill reps alone. Strangely, I couldn't find anybody to train with me. I got a few offers of company, but 100 per cent of them ended up being no shows.

After a night of riding the Wellington hills, I then had to get up and go to the gym first thing in the morning for spin classes – the ones with those stationary exercise bikes, where you can really wind up the resistance. And then I'd do extra workouts before and after. It was my first real attempt at proper training with someone knowledgeable guiding my effort.

At the time, Brad was helping a lot with fundraising for the PBP. At the gym there was a spin instructor, Craig Earles. Together with Brad, the pair was like a marketing machine at the gym. Brad was running a 'boot camp' at the time, providing merciless military-style physical training. He auctioned himself in a promotion called 'Train the trainer'. The 'grunts' in his boot camp threw money in a kitty and put in the highest bid.

They got their money's worth. In their 'training' they got Brad to eat two cold mince pies and drink a can of Coke and then exercise – all at seven in the morning. This guy was super healthy, and food like that wouldn't normally pass his lips. Even better, I got to watch. It was great entertainment. He raised $300 on that one.

As soon as he found out that I wanted to do the PBP, Craig was marketing me the whole time. From then on, at the spin class every Friday morning, he would sing my praises and promote my cause.

Local Wellington cycling shop Penny Farthing Cycles sponsored me with equipment for the PBP. Mike Searle, the Penny Farthing bike mechanic, got my cycle ready. I didn't know it then, but Mike would figure prominently in my upcoming racing.

In all my previous races, I just did everything myself, apart from driving the follow car, which often fell to Dianna and her dad. And my training would just be a bike ride from Ngaio to Palmerston North and back, 320 kilometres in total, to visit the family. But the PBP was 1200 kilometres, nearly twice the distance of my longest event, the Taupo Cycle Challenge Super Enduro. I would need to muster double the heart and endurance and, perhaps, even more than that.

There were five Kiwis, four guys and one woman, who qualified for the 2007 PBP. As well as me, the other qualifiers were Steve Sharpe, Colin Anderson, Douglas Mabey and Marian Savage.

You're not allowed any support from anyone on the PBP, except at checkpoints. For safety reasons, the support vehicles aren't even allowed on the same road as the riders. If the officials see a support vehicle anywhere other than where it should be, their rider is immediately disqualified.

Before the brevet, I did a 'cycling bus tour' of France with some Aussie guys who were all competing as well. The tour was a combination of sightseeing, cycling and training. We'd bus to different destinations that had great cycling routes, then jump on our bikes, which had been transported on the bus, and cycle away. This was fun and enlightening, because I got a feel for the country, and the Aussie guys were great value. I made some good friends there.

The PBP taught me some lessons for racing overseas. For example, we just assumed everything would be open in France on Sunday. The race started on a Sunday night and the essential pre-ride carbo-loading needed to be dealt with. This involved eating plenty of starchy, carbohydrate-rich food – pasta, rice, bread, potatoes. These carbs would be readily converted into glucose in the muscles while I rode. But no, everything was shut – there weren't supermarkets open, not even a corner shop.

The hotel we were staying in had no cooking facilities so we were quite limited with what we'd be able to eat anyway. Eventually, we found a service station superette that had some couscous that you could cook in boiling water. I don't even like couscous, but it was the best thing I could find.

The PBP began at eight o'clock that Sunday night, which seemed like a very odd start time to me. And it's a massive start – 5000 people in all. This huge number of riders surge out in three groups, depending on what time-limit group they're riding in. Those doing the race within an 80-hour time limit start first – this was the group I was in. Then there's the under-90-hour time limit group. After this comes the riders doing the ride in under 84 hours – this was the group that Steve Sharpe was in. The under-84-hour group started nearly a full day after the 80-hour riders.

As I've said, officially, this is not a race. The clock runs continuously, and from the beginning to the end you've got to go through all these checkpoints. You have a card that needs to be signed at each checkpoint and then you move on. You carry your own gear. You can stop and get food wherever you like, as long as you stop at the checkpoints and follow the route.

I've never been in such a big bunch before – it was like the crowd after a rugby test match, crammed together, all trying to leave through the same gate. We were all going into the night, rain was falling steadily, and it was the most aggressive start I've ever experienced. A heap of the older Italian and French riders stuck their elbows out, trying to knock other riders off the road.

So much for the friendly nature of this event – these guys were on me the whole time. They gave me no space, cut into any lines I was trying to find in the bunch, and I can absolutely confirm that the elbow is the hardest bone in the human body! This melee continued for the first 100 kilometres, and I was surprised that I survived without dropping my bike or crashing into someone else. It would have been an ugly tangle if I had toppled over. I was shitting myself.

To my relief, after 100 kilometres the bunch separated out a bit. The rain kept coming down and continued to do so for the first day or so. I was riding with a couple of guys from Denmark for a while and they were quite buoyant, cracking jokes and laughing, but as the rain continued to fall, their mood dropped. It didn't bother me in the slightest – it was just rain. The Taupo qualifier was harder than this! And then there had been my training ride to Tauranga . . .

Back in June, Dianna's nana in Tauranga was celebrating her ninetieth birthday. I thought, this is great, I can incorporate it with my training. The plan was to bike from Wellington, over the long, winding Rimutaka Hill to the Wairarapa, then through the Hawke's Bay region, right around the Gisborne coast before cutting back inland to Tauranga. The PBP wasn't until August and the European summer. This was in June, at the beginning of the New Zealand winter.

By the time I got to Dannevirke, a couple of hundred kilometres into the route, it was raining so hard that there was a thick sheet of water on the main road. I pulled into a service station for a coffee. It must have been a strange sight, a guy fully decked out in cycling gear, all the road lights flashing on his bike, drenched, walking in from the torrential rain and into the calm fluorescent glow of the servo shop. At least, I imagined it must have looked strange to the two cops standing at the counter. They asked where I was heading.

'Hawke's Bay's my next stop.'

'You going out in this?' one of them asked.

'Yep. I've got to make Tauranga in a day and a bit. It's my girlfriend's nana's ninetieth, so I better not miss that.'

They both looked at me in silence and shook their heads.

Just before I got to Hawke's Bay, Dianna caught up to me in the car, and we decided that the weather was so bad she should follow me. By the time we got to Hicks Bay, there were slips right across the road that we could barely get the car around. Water was gushing down gullies, rolling rocks and other debris in its wake.

Then, after we passed through Tokomaru Bay, a van started following us, just keeping the same speed as us, holding back. We didn't know what this person was doing, but it felt a bit creepy, like they were stalking us. There was nobody else out there on this wild night, just us . . . and the van. It finally took the turn-off to Ruatoria.

In one part of this trip, I had to jump in the car as the road was unrideable. There were slips everywhere, water and stones all over the road. Eventually we got to Tauranga but, because of the car ride, I was still 100 kilometres short of the distance I wanted to have done, so I cycled to Rotorua and back to make up a total of 1000 kilometres.

The PBP was easy weather-wise in comparison to that training ride. It wasn't cold. And the rain was constant, but not heavy.

For anyone contemplating long-distance cycling, this is a great event and a lot of fun. Generally older guys do it. If you just want to cruise and take your time and use all the ninety-odd hours you're allocated, you can. Just breeze along and soak up the party atmosphere. Because the PBP is one of the oldest cycling events in the world, it has a lot of history attached to it, and this is evident in the popular support it attracts. All the towns are lined with people. The French love their cycling, they're really passionate about it. They'll have food on the side of the road for you. I loved those steaming bowls of delicious soup.

The route went through some lovely parts of France and passed through beautiful, centuries-old villages. There were some wonderful sights. And then there were some not-so-wonderful sights . . .

At one point in the event, there was a bunch of us and we dropped over a hill. Then this campervan came over the hill, too, passed us and stopped at the side of the road. Out jumped a rider. He got on his bike and started cycling. He must have been German because there were a couple of other German riders with us who started yelling at him. I don't understand German, but their meaning was very clear. But this guy had no shame – he jumped out of the van, onto his bike and off he went. It was unbelievable to see such brazen cheating in a ride that wasn't supposed to be competitive.

The Paris–Brest–Paris was the first time I got an insight into how lack of sleep can affect riders. I saw other riders who were obviously hallucinating, off in some completely different reality. I was passing through a small village and there was an Italian guy wandering up and down, ranting and raving. He'd completely lost the plot.

Another time, I was sitting at a checkpoint and this little Asian guy came running in with no pants on. He had lost his cycle shorts somewhere. He was asking if anybody had any for sale, or any he could borrow. You don't wear underpants with cycle shorts. They have a little chamois inside that stops the sweat and the chafing. So, if you lose your shorts, you walk around naked. He had his top pulled down over his thighs and he was doing this little shuffle. Who knows what went on there? I could never figure it out.

I would have my own moments of embarrassment too. As the race progressed, I got really sick. It really hit me at the halfway mark in Brest. I was feeling a bit drained toward the end of this stage. Then the pains started. I found myself curled up on the concrete floor of a school hall that was being used as a checkpoint with these intense stomach cramps. I hadn't eaten anything or drunk anything for about three hours prior to that. I don't know what caused it – possibly bad water. I tried to keep an eye on where my water came from. But at one of the checkpoints, I was looking around and I didn't actually see where the race official filled my drink bottle. It could have been from a tap or a hose outside. On the other hand, there was lots of cow dung on the road and this could have splashed up onto my bottle.

The cramps developed into a really bad tummy bug and dysentery. Dianna was meeting me again at a checkpoint that was about 120 kilometres on towards Paris. This meant I had to bike back over the Brest Hill, which is one of the biggest climbs in the race. I ground out the kilometres, stopping every hour or so to go to the toilet. The road banked up on either side, so I couldn't conceal myself. Every rider and vehicle that passed could see what I was doing. It was a bit of a missed opportunity, though – I could've put my Australian top on and pretended I was an Aussie out there on the road taking a dump.

The silly thing about this is that I was wearing bibs, cycle shorts that have straps over the shoulders, so to go to the toilet, I had to take off my top layers to get to these. I was so tired and sick that it never occurred to me that I could've left them hanging down, and it would have been a lot easier. But no, I put them all back on, jumped back on the bike and about an hour later, oh no! I've got to go again. I couldn't eat, couldn't drink. I went a good ten hours without food and five hours without drinking. With my level of exertion, this could have begun to get dangerous.

Eventually I met up with Dianna at the checkpoint, where I curled up in the campervan and had a sleep. I was out for a good couple of hours. Then I managed to get down half a muesli bar.

I got back on my bike and slowly started to peck away at the other riders. Eventually I found that I could drink again. Slowly, I started to feel better and better. And I started to nail back one rider after another. I would catch up to a bunch and think, I'm going better than you guys, and would mow past them.

I don't know why, but I was feeling really good. Amazing, actually. I beat all the Australians that I'd started with, so that was satisfying.

The fastest Aussie guy wasn't feeling very good at the 400-kilometre mark. I rode with him up over into Brest. And that's when I got sick. He obviously recovered and he took off again. Where's the Anzac spirit in that? I didn't catch him until the very last stage. I saw him at a checkpoint, and he was looking really bad again. He left just before me. I was almost going to leave my backpack at the checkpoint to lighten my load, but luckily I didn't.

I wasn't back on the road for long when I went over a bit of steel and cut right through one of my tyres. I had to change it. And the handle of my pump had come loose – in fact, there was no handle on it, just a bit of metal sticking out. I kept waving guys down, saying, 'Have you got a pump?' But no one would give me one so I had to pump it with the bare shaft and it was cutting into my hand. After that I just rode with anger. And somewhere in the night I passed the Aussie guy. I got ahead of him by 15 minutes.

As I biked through the towns, I'd see riders huddled up in shop entranceways, trying to sleep. Colin Anderson told me that he'd slept in a goat hut somewhere in the middle of the countryside.

One of the other interesting things about the PBP is that the last quarter of it is ridden at night. I can't read French and didn't exactly know where I was going – these factors mixed in with a lack of sleep set off a slowly building panic.

I started to think I might have missed a direction change or that someone might have pulled a sign out. I had heard about riders going as much as 100 kilometres off course. I had no idea which was the right direction. I couldn't even guess which way Paris was. I was weaving through these small villages and towns in a country that I knew nothing about. I thought, if I get lost . . . And it happens to people every year, riders cycling way off course, lost in the dark, in an unfamiliar country, amidst exhaustion and sleep deprivation.

Just as I was really starting to panic, I saw the little red flashing tail light of a bike in front of me and the relief was immense, knowing that I was on the right track. Then I started hoping that the person in front of me wasn't lost . . .

I planned to complete the PBP in 55 hours; my final time was 60 hours. At the end, I finished the fastest Southern Hemisphere rider. I came 108th out of 5000. I reflected on the PBP, how I'd done in that. There's no doubt it's a race. There are records for it, and trophies are handed out. And it was my first real experience of riding with lack of sleep. That two hours I had in the campervan was probably enough to help me recover from sleep deprivation and give me enough rest to cope with the stomach upset.

That feeling of wellbeing I got halfway back to Paris must have been some sort of burst of survival energy, perhaps a physiological reaction to stress and illness. In truth, I was still sick. I had dysentery for ten days afterwards. I was sick on the plane trip home. And I had developed tendonitis in the Achilles tendon in my right foot. Tendons are made up of fibrous connective tissue. The Achilles is the strongest tendon in the body and connects the foot with the calf muscles. Mine now creaked when I walked.

It was at the PBP that I first heard about the Race Across America (RAAM). The RAAM is exactly what the name says it is – a race across America, covering some 4800 kilometres from the West Coast to the East Coast. It sounded amazing to me, a mind-blowing event. And I thought that maybe I could do it. I locked it away in the back of my mind. I knew, at that point in my racing career, that I wasn't ready. I might have been able to finish it, but I just didn't think I was mentally tough enough to do it at that point.

Going into the PBP, I imagined that there would be a wall that I would hit. That I would smack into it, and that would be the end of my effort. There would be nothing left. I would have no energy, I wouldn't have slept, my willpower would give out, my body would turn off, and I would just stop. On the PBP, I learned that there is no wall. I hit that place, and I would just work out a way to push through it. This was the point of mental toughness, the mind game that had to be played with endurance events. And I was good at it. One day I would get the RAAM in my sights.

Chapter 4

Making the cut

The injection of blood was directed into the area around my Achilles tendon. It sounds gruesome, and I guess it is. The other treatment options sounded more disturbing to me – dry needling, where a long needle is prodded straight into trigger points within the tendon, or straight-out surgery, where a series of small incisions are made in the tendon to stimulate blood flow.

This injection seemed like the best option. It's called an autologous blood injection. I had the procedure done at Wakefield Hospital in Wellington. The doctor took blood from my arm and injected it into my heel. The reason for having what sounds like a weird procedure was that the natural growth properties, primarily the platelets, in the blood help heal the tendonitis inflammation.

A lot of athletes end up with problems with their Achilles tendons, but this was the first time I'd experienced it. My tendon creaked like a dry old pair of shoes when I walked. And the sensation that my heel was packed full of ground glass was none too pleasant. It was an odd and horrible feeling.

My Achilles problem was the fallout from the PBP, that and quite a bit of weight loss. But I had to get sorted quickly if I wanted to be ready for the next Taupo Maxi Enduro. The tendonitis knocked off five weeks of training, which only left me another few months in which to train for the four-lap Taupo event. Blood injections don't work for everyone, but thankfully it worked for me. I just needed the one and I was ready for Taupo. Well, ready enough . . .

I had a good support crew for the 2007 Taupo Maxi Enduro. Dianna was there, as was Brad Quinn. He'd moved to Brisbane but flew back to New Zealand to crew for me for this race. Also on the team was someone else quite impor-tant who had come into my life: Phillip Beach, an osteopath and acupuncturist. He helped out with the aches and pains and bodily stresses. He and his partner, Robyn, brought their own vehicle to support me for this race.

There were about eight of us in a bunch on the first lap. Among them were Brad Sara, a younger rider who always looked the part – white lycra, tanned, with stylish riding glasses – and Thomas Lindup, whom I'd raced against in some of the 12-hour mountain-bike races – he was only in his early twenties and incredibly fast.

On the first lap, going into Hatepe Hill, Lindup attacked. As I've mentioned, the first part of the course has nearly all the hill climbs, then along comes Hatepe, about 135 kilometres into the circuit. Everyone held back, thinking, 'He won't last.' We never saw him again.

For the rest of the race, Brad, a guy from New Plymouth and I rode together. Coming up to the halfway mark on the last lap, I decided I had to get rid of these guys somehow. I got an energy drink from my support crew just before Kuratau Hill, sculled it back, rode a few minutes to let it digest, then attacked. It caught both of the other riders by surprise.

I saw Thomas Lindup again at the finish and he could barely walk. He looked pretty shot, but he took the gamble and it paid off. He absolutely smashed everyone – a fast rider, for sure, he went on to become the under-21 world champ for the 24-hour mountain-bike race.

Later I found out from Phil and Robyn that when they went 'off duty' to go for a sleep, they had come across Lindup in his final run to the finish line. Lindup had made an arrangement with his support crew that they could cycle with him after three laps. But the support guy who had all his food and drinks simply couldn't keep up. Feeling a bit sorry for Thomas, Robyn and Phil gave him some chocolate and some water. By then he had maybe 40 kilometres to go. But this was a race, and they were supposed to be on my crew! To be fair, Phillip did shout me an Emerson's pilsner at the finish so there was some compensation.

The following year, Dianna and I broke up. We'd been together for 12 years. Things hadn't been right for us for some time. We'd got together when we were both young, and as the years went on we began to grow apart. Cycling is quite a selfish sport, too, which I'm sure had something to do with it – the long hours of training and the competitions themselves were hugely time consuming. I think Dianna had the courage to say that it was time to call it quits, more so than me. A typical male thing, perhaps, trying to ignore what was right in front of my face.

Even in France, during the PBP, I could tell something was missing between us. We stayed in Paris, the most romantic city in the world, but we felt little sense of that. I put it down to being tired after the brevet.

We rented a little apartment in the centre of the city for a week, but couldn't find the motivation to go out and experience the city at night. We did the usual touristy things together – the Arc de Triomphe, the Louvre, the cathedral of Notre Dame, walking down the Champs-Élysées and beside the Seine. The view from the apartment took in an ancient fountain. It was full of a magical beauty, but held little magic for us.

At the time, it was hard to take – but like many partnership break-ups, after a while I could see that it was the best for both concerned.

That year, 2008, I won my first Taupo enduro.

Other things were changing in my life too. I had established a sponsorship deal with Penny Farthing Cycles in Wellington. One day as I walked out of Penny Farthing I bumped into Mike Searle on the street outside. He'd just begun a business as a mobile bike mechanic. He had converted a van into a workshop with every tool and spare you might ever need. He could deal with any eventuality on the road. He said that he'd like to sponsor me, but that he didn't have much money at the moment – but as things picked up, he'd give me a better deal.

I already had a good arrangement with Penny Farthing, who had offered me a slightly better agreement. But I turned that down and agreed to do a deal with Mike and Searletech. True to his word, in six months' time, his business picked up and my sponsorship got better. All my labour was free from him for all the bikes and I got wholesale prices on bikes and equipment.

The development of my racing career and Mike Searle building up his business went hand in hand for some time. He became a major part of my improving my pace, as he had a sharp approach to matching hardware to conditions. The equipment he supplied me was always the best.

I was really ready to race that year. One of the Australian mates I'd met on the PBP, Steve from Wagga Wagga, flew over to do the four-lap race at Taupo as well. He was a pretty fast bike rider. There were some other colourful characters competing too – Andrew Elliston, for example. Although using the word 'compete' is probably a bit of an exaggeration when it comes to talking about Andrew. He doesn't go in to win, he goes in to finish. He says it himself, that he's there to make up the numbers and make everybody else look good. Dave Comans was there, too. He was another guy I'd done a lot of riding with.

On the first hill of the first lap, I attacked. I wanted to get out in front and separate from everybody on that first lap. Dave Comans, Brad Sara and Steve from Wagga Wagga came with me.

The weather was good at the start, but it would gradually build to the sort of stifling heat that Taupo can turn on.

Halfway through the first lap Dave Comans said, 'Stuff this, it's meant to be an endurance race, not a sprint.' He dropped away. One thing I noticed was that Steve was eating solid food – the rest of us were on liquid food. I told Brad not to slow down at the top of each hill climb, because this was the only place Steve got a chance to eat. So every time we got to the top of a hill, Brad and I would pick up the pace. Then Steve would be shuffling around with his food and putting it back in his pocket without eating it. Eventually, he just faded. It was a mean thing to do to a friend – but all is fair in racing.

At the start of the second lap I picked up the pace again. I left Brad Sara vomiting on the side of the road. And I was virtually on my own for the rest of the race. About 60 kilometres from the finish my support crew came up and told me that Brad Sara was just behind me. They had talked about it and decided they weren't going to tell me until they absolutely had to. Sometime beforehand, they'd seen him come into the service station that's used as a checkpoint and he was looking remarkably fresh.

The adrenaline started kicking in – I thought it was going to be a sprint to the end. He never caught me. And, in fact, he was a bit further behind than I thought. I could only just see his support car when I looked around after I crossed the finish line.

I was now the person to beat on the Taupo enduros. I'd secured first place.

I built up a touring bike and went down to the South Island. It was my way of clearing my head after the break-up and having to sell the house that Dianna and I had owned together. I spent six weeks in March and early April, pinning back big tours, riding every day and sightseeing. The South Island has some spectacular scenery, the Southern Alps, rough coastlines of harsh beauty, calendar-perfect farmland. Towards the end of this tour, I was nailing back 200 kilometres a day — on a fully loaded touring bike.

Needless to say, I was getting quite fit. I was halfway through the tour when I got a call from Mike, my new sponsor. He said, 'I've got you a new mountain bike.' Well, that's okay, I thought. Then I got a call when I was near the bottom of the South Island, in Invercargill. He said, 'I've entered you into the Moonride 24-hour mountain-bike race in May.' I said, 'Yeah, cool.'

During the rest of the tour, I kind of let this slip my mind. But that's what this tour was all about — letting go, clearing my heart, a kind of peaceful forgetting.

When I finally got back to Wellington, Mike and I started flatting together. He presented me with this hot mountain bike. The only thing was, I didn't have much time to train for this 24-hour mountain-bike event. I rode the bike three or four times before I did the race. It was enough.

During the cycle tour, I had built up a sort of steely fitness. I was incredibly strong on the bike. I had changed physically too, becoming leaner in my upper body. But 24 hours non-stop was still a daunting prospect. I went as hard as I could. At one point, I broke a bike chain during the race and had to run half a lap of the 8-kilometre circuit, pushing my bike beside me. The guys coming first and second overtook me because of this gear failure.

When I got back to base, I threw my bike down for Mike to fix. As well as being my main sponsor, he'd instigated a professional approach to crewing for me and was on my crew for this event. His van was there as a support vehicle with all the spares and tools and, of course, there was Mike. He was an exceptional mechanic – and fast. I was back up on the bike in no time and I mowed down everyone in front of me.

Standing in the winner's spot on the podium after completing 56 laps, the guy who came second said to me, 'We were waiting for you to stop, but you didn't. You just kept on going.' Most riders usually stop to get food, but I just kept going and going. I was astonishingly fit after that tour and something had changed in me. There was a new resolve and my competitive streak had hardened into something irreducible, something solid and unyielding.

After Brad Quinn had left for Australia, I needed to find another trainer to replace him. Shane Tindall from Specific Training took over where Brad had left off. And he kept working on my core. I liked his style of training. A bit of a drill sergeant, Shane really drove me along. Phillip Beach repaired me every time I was broken and Shane kept me physically strong.

Then it was back to Taupo for the four-lap race again. That was my year to race against Peter Cole. We'd had a year where we hadn't competed against each other, but he was back on the start line. He'd begun the Taupo race the year before, in 2008, but had pulled out after the second lap with dehydration – it was a real heat ride and he hadn't had enough fluids on the first lap.

In this Taupo race, there was only me, Peter Cole and Brad Sara in the leading bunch. The first lap was really fast, an absolute blinder, faster than most people do the single-lap event. We'd just gone through Turangi, heading toward the sinuous road that winds around beside the lakeshore.

It was a fiercely hot day, but we were all pushing up the pace. We were in single file – Peter was in front, then me, and Brad was on my tail. We must have been doing 40 kilometres an hour as we drilled down on the pedals. A ute pulled out and overtook us all, then abruptly turned in front of us, nearly coming to a stop as it turned into a driveway.

Pete was down on his 'aero' bars, the ones you lean onto over the front wheel. He just went smack! face-first into the back of the car. I hammered on my brakes and flew over the handlebars, sliding onto the road. Then Brad crumpled sideways behind us.

That old cliché that 'everything happened quickly' is so true. I was a bit stunned. My support crew went to help out Pete. He was a huddled heap on the road, with blood coming out of every joint. I knew right then that his race was over. Meanwhile, one of the guys in the support crew had run after the guy in the driveway. I thought there was going to be a brawl.

I'd grazed my knees and elbows and shoulders. I was sort of all right, full of adrenaline, and completely focused on the race. I said to my crew, 'Where's my spare bike? Let's keep going here, we've got to keep up this lead on the first lap!' I didn't want to lose that. Brad Sara was all right, too. He'd just injured a hand landing.

That year, I probably had one of my best support crews: Mike Searle, Shane Tindall and Greg Hart. Nothing was a hassle with the crash. The bike got sorted out and everything was done. Everything just ran like clockwork. I was back onto the bike in minutes.

By this stage I was pissed off, really angry. The crash had incensed me. I rode really hard. I thrashed the pedals. After the crash, I was gone. I didn't see anyone again until the finish line. I absolutely smashed Brad – my next biggest rival after Peter Cole.

Coming in on the second lap, everyone was suffering from the heat. I was feeling overheated too. A headache was starting to brew in my brain and my gut felt heavy, like I'd swallowed a bag of raw potatoes. When we came to the top of Hatepe Hill, I stopped and told my support crew that I was feeling crook. Then I threw up. Instantly, I felt much better. 'All good now,' I said to the crew. 'Let's get going.' I got back on my bike and ripped into the race.

Pete was really bad. We had to fill out police reports the next day. I felt bad for him. He had a young family and had spent all that time training, just for some guy in a ute to take all that away from him. Pete's goal had been the same as mine – he wanted to qualify for the RAAM. We were on the same path at that stage.

The car that cut us off had been driven by a young guy. He had been drinking but he wasn't over the limit – he'd just had a couple of beers at lunch. What he didn't realise was how fast we were going – he'd misjudged our speed and made a stupid mistake.

Aside from the injuries to his body, Pete sustained $14,000 of damage to his bike. The damage to my bike, clothes and wheels was close to four thousand.

�🚲

There was another four-lap Taupo race in 2009 at which I took line honours. After that, Pete and I were both serious about getting into the RAAM. We discussed how we could get a qualifier in New Zealand.

We both joined the Ultra Marathon Cycling Association in order to find out the process of getting a race recognised as a RAAM qualifier. And we tried to involve Keith Crate, the organiser for the Taupo races, too. The RAAM qualifier ended up being one of the most gruelling Lake Taupo races ever and one of the toughest rides of my life.

As soon as the Taupo race was confirmed as a qualifier, the stakes suddenly went up. It was quite an important one for me. This qualifier was also going to be a test of endurance mettle – eight punishing laps of Lake Taupo, 1280 kilometres. We knew that there were going to be about 20 people in the race, but at that stage only Peter Cole and I were using it as a qualifier for the RAAM.

I'd gone as far as I could with training on my own. Brad Quinn and Shane Tindall had been great as my gym coaches, and had really raised my performance, but now I needed to step up a level and have a dedicated cycling coach. I knew I had to pick up the speed for this sort of racing, and that required proper, targeted training with someone who specialised in coaching individual athletes for specific and, in my case, extreme events.

A year out from the RAAM, and five months before the qualifier, I enlisted the help of Silas Cullen from Smart Coaching. I'd met Silas a couple of times before this. He'd help do 'bike fits' with me, making sure that my bikes were set up to get the best benefit for the energy I expended, but also to give my body the least stress.

Silas was perfect for my needs. He's an experienced and highly educated coach with a passion for enduro events. Thoughtful, positive and incisive, he helped hone my endurance and prepared me for both the qualifier and the RAAM. A line on his website summarises his approach: 'The harder you think, the faster you go.' Silas is no slouch on a cycle himself. He came second in the New Zealand national road champs in 2012.

Silas has an online system. You fill in a log each day, which he then responds to. If you get sick, or there's something else to take into account, he can change your programme immediately.

The coaching presented a challenge for him as the qualifying event, the eight-lap race around Taupo and the RAAM required quite different, almost opposite, coaching regimes. We discussed many of the issues that the two races presented. From Silas's point of view, he would have much preferred that I was doing more conventional racing than the Taupo Extreme Enduro prior to the RAAM.

He pointed out that when you build up for any event, the principle of specificity is the most important. You start out non-specific and get more specific. So, say for a conventional race, like once around Lake Taupo, he'd start off with the long stuff, building up endurance, then do more bunch riding – shorter, harder, more intense rides. About two weeks before the race he would schedule in a really hard race, or a concentrated training session, to lift the intensity further.

Building up to the RAAM, it would have made more sense to work on speed first, then try to hold some of that speed through the later endurance training. But this approach was impossible because of the timing of the qualifying race. And it was important for me that I nail that qualifier. It was a key race for me. It gained a further edge when I found out that the owner of the RAAM, Fred Boethling, was coming over from Boulder, Colorado to see the race.

Fred is a guy with a generous smile and an easy American manner. He's an ultra-cycling legend. This businessman, mountaineer and adventurer set the over-60 team record with Dan Crain in 2005 for the race that he administered. At 61, he became the oldest solo cyclist to finish the RAAM.

Peter Cole and I approached Fred before we did the 2010 qualifier in Taupo to confirm that there was to be no drafting allowed. As we understood it, those were RAAM rules, and Fred verified that this was the case. We were the only ones who didn't draft during the qualifier.

This race was going to be the big showdown between Pete and me. The way we each went about our build-up highlighted our different approaches and personalities. Pete asserted his confidence in several ways. There were magazine articles that discussed how he was training, promoting him as a strong contender for the race. He talked as if he'd already qualified. I wasn't so sure about things.

I tended to go about training in my own way. He was all set to go to the RAAM, whereas I wasn't really prepared. And I wasn't going to organise anything until I qualified. That's just the way I work. This stance aggravated my crew.

The crew was probably the most dedicated, well-organised and slick to date. Robyn Pearce was crew chief. A highly organised woman, she would go on to make a massive contribution to fundraising and the organisational build-up to the RAAM. Robyn was married to Phillip, my osteopath. He was the recovery champion in the team. He manipulated away aches, strains, pains and misalignments. He kept my body in good condition and injury free. He was also a good beer-drinking buddy, with a taste for craft beers.

Phil and Robyn had been a major part of my life after I'd broken up with Dianna. I'd stayed with them for a while after that and they were generous in their support and friendship.

Shane Tindall as my gym trainer was on board, as was Greg Hart. Greg had been a rally car navigator and served on the support crew for rally cars. He had a keen sense of the logistical set-up of crewing and the need for speed in interactions with the racer. There was Mike Searle, a sharp, fast bike mechanic. And someone else had come into my life, Michelle Cole. She helped out with food requirements – she had studied nutrition, so had a good handle on the best foods for high-output exercise.

Mike had 'introduced' us. He gave me a ring one day and said, 'Do you want to take this girl out for a ride? She's training for the Coast to Coast.' And that was fine, I'd tagged along on plenty of rides and runs with other people to learn the ropes.

She hadn't done much road cycling but was a good mountain biker, and fit. Road cycling is a bit different from mountain biking, as I'd discovered earlier, so I was happy to help out. Small-framed and trim, she proved to be a bit of a dynamo on the bike. I liked her attitude. She had a flinty determination, a single-minded focus.

I suggested that she should come out riding with Andrew Elliston and me. There's always a joker in every pack, and Andrew's one of them. And, for some reason, Andrew and Michelle ended up sitting on my rear wheel and razzing me the whole way. They took great delight in bantering and making jibes at my expense. My ears were burning the whole time we were on the road – I couldn't always make out what they were saying. These were great rides, fun and invigorating.

We ended up doing a 300-kilometre ride, from Wellington to the Wairarapa and back again. And later, a 500-kilometre Opperman. An Opperman is a fun event. Riders from different locations ride to a common destination with the proviso that they do this in a single day and cover at least 400 kilometres.

I felt an affinity with Michelle – we both enjoyed the same sort of sport and we enjoyed each other's company. I was a bit slow on the uptake – I wasn't sure if she was that keen on me. It took me a while to click that the attraction was mutual.

The crew was definitely strong, and this was probably the reason they spoke up on the issue of the RAAM. They thought that, like Pete, we should have been putting our campaign together, getting sponsors, looking into our strategy for when we'd be in the States. If we didn't do that now, and if I qualified, we would be playing catch-up the whole way. They thought I should be getting everything sorted as if I was going. But I didn't want to know about it. My view was that I hadn't qualified yet and, until I had, I wasn't going. There was a sequence of things in my mind. And that's how it was.

My goal was to show everyone how fast I am, to beat everyone convincingly in the Taupo Extreme Enduro. Not just to win, but to win well. Then, and only then, I'd get the RAAM squarely in my sights. But until I'd trounced the field in the qualifier, I wasn't ready, I wasn't worthy and I hadn't qualified.

Whereas Pete had organised a crew, publicity, gear. He had all the flash stuff done. I heard he'd even had T-shirts printed.

The qualifying race was set for the end of November, and it was a fine day. The heat built as the day wore on into one of those oppressively hot, still Taupo days. On the first lap, there were a few of us together for a little while. My strategy was to keep an eye on Pete and see what he was doing.

Pete made a few comments when we were going over the first series of hills, saying that he thought the pace might have been a bit quicker. We were going at it pretty hard. This was an obvious ruse on his part to cause a little psychological uncertainty. I was unperturbed.

For this qualifier, I had a time-trial bike that I'd never used in a race before. After we'd done all the hilly parts and hit the long, flat stretch through Turangi, I wanted to switch to the time-trial bike and have a burst on it. What was strange was that Pete was using a time-trial bike the whole way. These bikes are heavily geared and are ideal for level stretches of road where you can get down low and really wind up the energy.

Mike and I were wondering why he was using this bike on the hills. I was relaxed doing hill climbs. Pete was struggling, putting the effort into the big gears. I didn't pay that much attention at the time as I was concentrating on the race. But the crew following behind said they could see it straight away. He was struggling up the hills whereas I was looking relaxed, spinning the pedals faster in lower gears.

When I stopped to swap bikes, Pete went past. He must have wondered what we were doing. I went from my normal bike to my time-trial bike. About ten kilometres down the road, I flew past Pete like he was standing still. I didn't say a word to him, just blasted past. My crew saw him look up, then slump over the handlebars. He was beaten right then and there. I didn't let up after that.

The Taupo circuit is not the place to use a time-trial bike the entire time. Pete just fell apart. He got back on his training bike in the end, struggling around. It was devastating for him but, in the end, it was a bad strategy. You make your choices in situations like that, and you've got to live with the consequences . . .

From then on, I started lapping people, one after the other. Some I ended up lapping twice. But it wasn't all easy. I went through a lot of pain at one stage. My Achilles began to bite on the third lap, and I was worried that I wasn't going to get through the pain. Silas and I had worked on conditioning the Achilles and talked about altering my foot position on the pedal, if necessary, so there would be less stress on this crucial tendon. I pushed on and my heel came right in the end.

My uncle lives in Kuratau – he works on a big farm there. Each lap, the family would be standing out at their farm gate, cheering me on – it didn't matter what time it was. My nana was especially staunch on being out there. She gave my crew strict instructions to text her an hour before I was coming through so she had time to get out to the gate. My auntie was usually there, too. And sometimes my uncle, if he wasn't working.

My grandad usually came up to support me when I raced in Taupo but he'd had a fall and was in hospital. He wanted me to finish the race – and win it – on his birthday. The race started on Wednesday and Grandad's birthday was on Friday. I finished on Friday night at around 9.30pm, so I cut it a bit fine.

On the last lap, I started to suffer. I began hallucinating through lack of sleep and rest. I stopped for one sleep of around ten minutes for the whole race. As I was riding, I could see all these pot plants lining the hills around Taupo as I passed them. Not grass or bush, but row upon row of pot plants. I came to a sudden halt at one point, convinced I'd seen a cellphone and wallet on the road. I picked them up. It was a piece of rubber sheared off a truck tyre. And once, I was certain I had seen the Loch Ness monster in the lake itself.

The next day, my old mate from school, Dion, turned up at my door and said, 'You weren't hallucinating – they were all over the hills.' He then presented me with a pot-plant pot replete with weeds. This wasn't the first stunt he'd pulled in relation to that race. On one of the laps, during the stifling heat of the day, he appeared on the side of the road kitted out in a wetsuit and flippers, shaking a bottle filled with stones. The next lap, he had his pants around his ankles and was bent over showing his bare buttocks. As I took in this picturesque sight, Dion shouted, 'It's a bike stand, bro!'

I still have the pot-plant Dion gave me. The weeds are flourishing. I realised later that I'd probably had hallucinations on other rides – the Tauranga training ride for the PBP, for example. At the dawn of that morning, I thought the whole road was covered in worms. Dianna said I was trying to dodge them. And I thought all the worm juice was spurting all over my face. There probably were worms on the road, but not as many as I perceived there to be.

I went straight into an ambulance after the finish line of the qualifier. The ambulance officers tested my glucose. I was close to being in diabetic shock. They gave me glucose gel and a lolly and told me to get something decent to eat. My next stop would be the pizza parlour with my crew and several meat-lover's pizzas.

I'd finished the race, all 1280 kilometres of it, in 55 hours. The second-place getter had come in over 12 hours behind me. I had completely blown away the entire field. I needed to do this to prove to myself that I was ready and capable of the RAAM. It's a much longer race with faster riders, riders faster than me. But now I knew I could do it.

After the race, people wanted to know the secret of how I'd got so fast. There was no secret. I had a good coach and a good support team who put lots of time and effort into me. I'd been guided into training in better ways and with better bikes.

Peter Cole had pulled out of the RAAM qualifier. His knee gave out. It had become too sore for him to continue.

And then came the kicker. At the Endurance Breakfast the next morning, Fred Boethling said that everyone who completed the eight laps of the Taupo race had qualified for the RAAM! Pete would have been spewing. I know he would have crawled around the course and finished if he'd known that was to be the outcome. I was the only one who qualified in the time allowance and who didn't draft in accordance with the RAAM rules. I was really pissed off.

I'd spent all that time and effort and then I saw a lot of people get a free ride. It seemed to level my effort to that of everybody else's. I had pushed myself really, really hard in the dream of being the first Kiwi to ride solo in the RAAM. That dream evaporated in an instant.

Ron Skelton, therefore, qualified and did the RAAM the same year as I did it. I shouldn't really be angry about it, and I could see Fred's point of view – he wanted to get more riders at the start line, to make the race bigger. I could have done the qualifier a lot easier but probably I wouldn't have . . .

My focus didn't so much change as shift: I wouldn't be the first Kiwi solo rider in the RAAM, but I was now determined to be the first Kiwi solo rider to finish it.

Chapter 5

Revving up for the RAAM

The RAAM would be the longest race of my life, approaching four times the distance I'd raced before. In practical terms, there was no way I could replicate this race in training. The best I could do was prepare myself.

And pray.

I worked intensively with Silas Cullen on the training programme, bike set-up and nutrition testing for this enduro-hell. 'The harder you think, the faster you go.' That motto from Silas's website held true for his approach as he devised a training strategy.

We talked a lot about the race and Silas put hours of thought into it.

The problematic thing isn't the distance, but that it's nonstop. Anyone with a bit of stamina and willpower could cycle that far – if they had enough time, rest and sleep. Sleep deprivation is the killer. It is by far the most punishing part. It sucks your will to continue as surely as if you had the blood drained from your body.

There are cyclists who, I know, can put out more wattage than me in a tour. But toughing it out through the lack of sleep, that brings a nightmarish dimension to the endurance mix. This is the difference between the RAAM and more classic cycle races – the Tour de France, for example.

The Tour guys are racing through every stage. They're clipping along at pace in big pelotons, battling it out over hills, sprinting in for split-second finishes. It's in 200-kilometre stages – shorter, sharper, faster racing. But then they have time for recovery. They have rest days. And they get to sleep.

The RAAM, like the Paris–Brest–Paris, or indeed our own Taupo Cycle Challenge Extreme Enduro, is continuous. Only four times longer. With the first part through the Mojave Desert . . .

As the days push on in a race like this, you cycle into an increasingly depleted state. The exertion wears down your physical energy and the sleep deprivation saps willpower. You get lazy. You mightn't be bothered eating. There could be food in your back pocket, but the *thought* of actually reaching back there and grabbing it is too much. This is the central nervous system winding down. Begging for sleep. It's a slippery slope. Perhaps you're not drinking enough electrolytes as a result of your tiredness, which means you're cycling into kidney failure.

Remember, your crew is tired, too – they've been awake a long time, or with very broken sleep, seeing to your needs as well as their own. If they miss something simple but crucial for your wellbeing, you won't be riding on a bike but in an ambulance.

The desert has the biggest attrition rate for solo riders – heatstroke, dehydration, kidney failure. One year, a solo rider had his father in the follow vehicle. This dad watched as his son's lower back swelled and swelled as his kidneys closed down. His ride ended in hospital. Fortunately, he recovered.

The race went 21 years without casualties. Then it had two fatalities. In 2003 Brett Malin, a team cyclist, did a U-turn at night on the crest of a hill outside of a town in New Mexico. An 18-wheeler truck-trailer unit topped the hill and took him out. Two years later, Bob Breedlove, a very experienced ultra-marathon cyclist, started swerving erratically at a point near Trinidad, Colorado. He slumped over his handlebars and veered into the path of an oncoming pickup truck.

And there have been any number of accidents, some very serious. In 2010 a Spanish rider, Diego Ballesteros Cucurull, was paralysed from the waist down after being hit by a car near Wichita, Kansas.

People raised questions about whether fatigue played a part in these events. There were suggestions that the race should have enforced rest periods. But those closest to the race eventually believed that this would undermine the essential nature of the race – that is, the mental and physical challenge of going nonstop across the country and being the first past the finish line.

My training was very measured. As Silas pointed out, he never wanted to put me into a state where I couldn't train for a month.

Training traditionally, you overload the body then you back off, then you overload it again and back off again. As you come closer to the event the training becomes more specific and harder, then you taper off and do the race. The training mimics what you'll actually do when you take off from the start and cross the finish line. But with something like the RAAM you can't do that. If you tried to simulate it too closely, you'd be so tired from the simulation that you would need months to recover. Far more would be lost in fitness than would be gained.

Instead, it's about addressing the structure of what will happen through each day – the nutrition, cycling into the night, the long stretches of sustained effort – pushing things as far as possible without having too much recovery after each key phase. The idea is to get as fit as you can and simulate things as closely as you can without getting so knocked around you can't compete.

People talk about motivation being a factor in how well you do in the race. And, of course, it is. But motivation is in your personality, it's ingrained. Some people have got the sort of character where they can push their body and mind to the limit and some people don't.

So, to counter something like sleep deprivation, the best thing to do is strike a balance between the central nervous system being robust and ready to go – 'topped up' is Silas's phrase – and fitness being carefully maintained through the last month of training. The taper-off of training is much longer for an ultra-marathon, even to the point that there's a possibility of feeling lethargic on the first day because you haven't really ridden that much. This comes back as a benefit in the last days of the race.

A sign of things to come—me on my first bike at 11 months old, at home in Otaki.

There's me, second from the right in the front row of the Cloverlea Primary School soccer team. I was nine years old and I made $1 for each goal I scored that season.

Me and Marie Kapluggin attending to a rugby player as St John cadets in Palmerston North.

My twenty-first birthday cake in the shape of a Jack Daniels bottle.

Having a beer and a smoke at my brother Kane's wedding, 21 January 2001, the night I told everyone I was going to do the Coast to Coast.

Crossing the Mahinga River during the 33-kilometre mountain run over Goat Pass during the Coast to Coast, February 2004.

Paddling the Waimakariri River during the Coast to Coast, February 2004.

In the finishing chute of the Coast to Coast—Sumner Beach, Christchurch, February 2004.

Eating steak, fries with mayonnaise, bread rolls and creamed rice at a checkpoint during the Paris–Brest–Paris brevet in France, 2006.

At the Villaines-la-Juhel checkpoint during the Paris–Brest–Paris brevet, 2006.

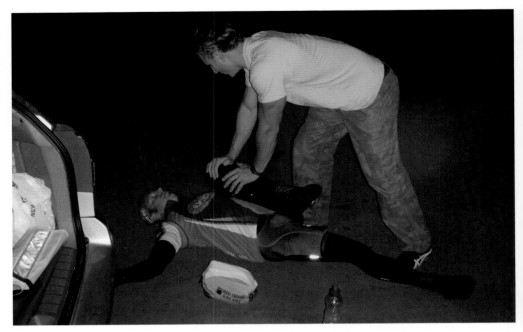

Brad Quinn stretching me out after three laps of the Taupo Maxi
Enduro 640-kilometre cycle race, November 2007.

Heading up Hatipi Hill on the last lap of the Taupo Maxi Enduro,
November 2009.

Grabbing a ten-minute sleep in the grass on the western side of Lake Taupo during the Extreme Enduro 1280-kilometre cycle race, November 2010.

Battling the early morning fog on the western side of Lake Taupo during the 2010 Extreme Enduro.

Having my blood glucose levels tested in the ambulance at the end of eight laps of the Extreme Enduro 2010.

My Taupo Extreme Enduro 2010 support crew. Left to right: Robyn, Mike, me, Michelle, Phil, Shane and Greg.

Although the Taupo Extreme Enduro had given me a taste of what it would be like, I would have to wing the mental toughness on the day. Silas and I agreed that there were a lot of unknowns going into the RAAM.

We spent a lot of time on my bike set-up, making it very upright. This was about preserving the back. If I got a sore back, my race would be over. The less stress there was to be on my back and my hamstrings, the more upright I needed to be on the bike. And I could afford to be more upright because the aerodynamics weren't as important at the speed I'd be cycling. And, in the end, it wouldn't matter how aerodynamic I was if I had screaming pain in my back or my hamstrings were cramping. So we unloaded the back.

Silas got me into a posture where my spine was in a 'neutral' position, with the lumbar curve – the inward curve of the lower back – where it would be naturally. In that position on the bike, I'd last to the finish line. If I tried to go too low, or slightly hunched, my back would get very sore. In ten days, it would be agonising if my spine wasn't in a supported position. That's how we set up the bike, not with anything to do with the muscles firing well, or making it aerodynamic, or any of the things we would normally look at before a race.

Silas thought the eight laps around Taupo were too close to the RAAM. There was a possibility that I wouldn't be fully recovered, for one thing, especially as I'd gone so hard. But the real issue was that it was a mere six months between events and this wasn't long enough for the sort of build-up I needed in the training. If we had a longer period to play with, the training could have been harder but I would still have had ample recovery time.

Given the limited time, it was just five weeks after Taupo that the training got hard again. And then, it was just over two months before solid work kicked in – three eight-hour rides in a row.

Because the race is such low intensity – that is, it's a regular pace for ten days and there are no sprints and no stages where it's necessary to pour on the energy – there wasn't a lot of intensity training needed. Silas had said that if he put intensity in my programme it would detract from something else – essentially the amount of cycling I could do.

The amount of detail he took into consideration for my training programme surprised me. He questioned me about my job as a plumber, taking into account that I'm pretty much on my feet all day. He even factored in that I moved house at one point during the build-up. I thought, 'Well, I'm shifting, but how much should that interfere with my workouts?' But these are all things that 'load' me, that take up time and energy. He would subtract that from the training equation and work with the time and energy that remained. So shifting house or having a big job on could push me over the edge and into depletion. These things needed to be factored into my training schedule.

The intensity was pretty much the same for everything, although Silas gave me two key sessions of four ten-hour rides in a row in what he called a 'broken-down simulation' of the event. What he meant by that was that these mirrored the race, but in miniature. And there was a sleep break between each day of the simulation. This was building up to a pretty hard effort.

These simulations were done four weeks out and seven weeks out. This gave three-and-a-half weeks of recovery. The week after the last simulation, I was to do three 60-minute easy rides. Travel time to get to the RAAM was a week, so there was no training there. Over in Oceanside, the starting point of the RAAM, Silas had programmed two two-hour rides and a three-hour ride. And then another three 60-minute rides. The training was to be very light while I waited for the race to start.

I think Silas got a bit concerned about the programme, especially when he delivered the part that had eight ten-hour rides. He described it as a form of torture, but then that's what the event is – putting your mind and body on the rack, then stretching them until you think they're going to snap, then stretching them some more. He asked, 'Is that all right? Are you okay with this?' I responded, 'If it's not, if I can't get through this, then I'm probably training for the wrong event.' Then I had another thought and asked, 'Do you think it's going to be enough?'

☙❧

With extreme or ultra endurance cycling, you've really got to be in tune with being on your own for a long time and actually enjoy that. All cyclists do to a degree, but what probably makes ultra enduros different is not only the ability to just keep going but to persist even in that state of separation that extreme exhaustion and sleep deprivation create.

Still, I've had a lot of training partners and riding buddies over the years. It can be a lot of fun when you're flying along the road and chatting or bantering. Andrew Elliston has been a great riding partner down the years. And Michelle has joined us many times and upped the ante in how much fun these rides could be.

I only really stopped riding with these two when I began training under Silas for the RAAM qualifier. This wasn't out of choice but necessity. Everything I did was at a set pace, at a set rate. This made group training rides difficult. I found that I couldn't concentrate on what I was meant to be doing if I rode with someone else. My heart rate wasn't at the right level, for example, or my cadence wasn't fast enough. I quite enjoyed these lone training sessions, however. I was training in a new, exciting way and for a race I was determined to do.

Silas and I discussed the strategy for the race. People who tend to win are those who sleep the least – it's not necessarily about the fastest average speed.

In the four ten-hour rides, Silas had instructed me to go hard on the first one, go as hard as I could for the whole ten hours. 'The start's real hard, just bang! you're gone,' he said. And the next few days was about easing effort, getting used to the regularity of output.

In the last day, I was to build again. But the main emphasis was about going hard on the first day, which sounds really crazy. But if you go easy on the first day it doesn't seem to affect how fast you go five days later. You might as well start out really hard. After 24 hours, riders tend to settle into a pace comparable with each other. Then it comes down to the person who sleeps the least.

It's the opposite of how someone would approach running a marathon. You don't go out as hard as you can in an event like that. This would have a huge effect on the rest of the race because you're working at a much higher intensity throughout.

So the last part of the training programme was about fine-tuning the trade-off between losing fitness through the three weeks of the taper off and having enough speed in the legs to hammer the first part of the event. The longer your taper, the fresher you feel, but the more fitness you lose and the less speed you have at the beginning where it's important to explode out at the start.

Chapter 6

The wheels fall off

'Mate, you've got some problems. You've got problems with your crew.' This is something I definitely didn't want to hear. When I got back to Wellington a week after the RAAM qualifier, I caught up with a friend and he delivered this grave assessment of the support crew. These were the people who were supposed to accompany me to the United States. And I thought, 'What am I going to do here?'

Different people pulled out for different reasons – personality clashes, disagreements and money. The eight-lap qualifier in Taupo acted as a try-out for how the crew would function in the RAAM. They worked in two shifts, with one crew on while the other rested or slept. We were testing out how this would fit together organisationally. In that crew was

Robyn Pearce, Phillip Beach, Mike Searle, Shane Tindall, Greg Hart and Michelle Cole.

Taupo unearthed all the issues I'd been oblivious to. I knew there were a couple problems that had been going on for a while. But almost the entire crew crumbling to pieces while I was training intensively, being stretched as thin as rice paper financially, working flat out on the days that I could, and helping out with organisational matters, too – this was a shock.

I gave December as the final date for withdrawing from the campaign.

A couple of the crew pulled out for purely practical reasons. Greg and Shane knew that it was unlikely they could crew – they would both have come if they could. Shane's a solo dad with two kids. Greg was going into a new job, and coming to the States would have meant at least four weeks off work.

If we could've afforded his flights, Greg would have come. Because the money was so tight for the RAAM campaign, each crew member had to pay for their own flight to the States. If I could have paid for everyone, I would have. But the money wasn't there. Final decisions drifted on into the new year.

One of the biggest problems crew-wise resulted from what was, perhaps, a deep-seated misunderstanding. This became a painful and troubling clash between me and my friend, flatmate and sponsor, Mike Searle. We saw things in completely different ways.

In the end, it came down to money. He thought that he would be given tickets to get to America and then be paid as my mechanic while there. This was because of all the time and effort he'd put in beforehand – getting bikes, servicing them, acting as my mechanic during races. All I could say to him was that there was no money. The campaign was being paid for out of my back pocket, and with what could be raised through sponsorship and what I could personally borrow.

Mike used to work at Penny Farthing Cycles, my former sponsor. He left Penny Farthing and started his own bike business, then offered to sponsor me. It wasn't till the countdown to the RAAM that the relationship hit a snag.

One of the most harrowing incidents for me was when he raised this issue at one of our crew meetings. He showed the monetary side of everything he'd done, detailing the bikes, the spares, the hours of labour he'd put in. This was not only painful for me, but humiliating. I asked him what price he would put on all the clients he'd got because of me, how much money had that earned him? He replied that he still had to work for that money. I wondered what this had to do with it – it was his business, and he'd been building this up the whole time I'd been racing.

I certainly wasn't making any money out of being on a bike. I came to realise that he considered the RAAM our dream. But it was *my* dream. I was the one out there biking it and racing it. His dream was to build up his business, and that's where his time and effort went. He couldn't see where our two aspirations met in the middle. There was no formal arrangement between us, no contract had been written up.

As to me paying for his airfares and time, I just said, 'No. I need a crew of five, not one.' I would have been happy to pay for everybody's flights, *if* I'd had the money. But he seemed to think I should be paying for his flights before anyone else's. He couldn't see that I put the same amount of importance on a chief and a medic as I did on a bike mechanic, and I think that was hurtful to him.

Around this time, Mike said to me, 'Why don't you just do it next year?' I was speechless. Mike knew why I was pushing to do it in 2011, that I had wanted to be the first Kiwi to be in the RAAM. That's why I had trained so hard the previous year to qualify for the upcoming race. He now knew that other New Zealand riders had signed up for it. I wasn't going to be the first Kiwi to enter it, so I wanted to be the first Kiwi to finish, to come in ahead of the others.

We had a get-together with a mutual friend in order to sort it out. But after a couple of hours of discussion and debate, our friend concluded that we were never going to agree.

I wondered what was driving this change in attitude in Mike, why he thought he should be getting more for his sponsorship.

Here, in New Zealand, he'd got a lot of exposure for his business. He helped me out with races all around the country. I was in a lot of magazines and numerous promotional situations – and there was Mike's van following me, capturing some of that attention directed at me. I thought that was the pay-off.

The RAAM was a separate thing from New Zealand. I didn't really see it this way until later, until I looked back on it after I'd finished the race. We were muddling the two things together, but they should have been treated as two completely different beasts. This was something we should have defined right at the beginning of our sponsorship arrangement: What are its parameters, what is supplied and what is given in return? These expectations hadn't been thrashed out from the start.

I've learned a lot through all this. Put an agreement in place, establish clarity in the relationship and everyone will know where they stand. If you define these things at the beginning, you're not left picking up the pieces at the end.

People who were close to me knew how stressed I was getting trying to deal with the crew. I'm not the best at dealing with people in the first place. I didn't want to fix all these issues. I just thought, 'Why can't they sort it out themselves?'

The money side of things was enormously stressful. The global recession had hit sponsorship everywhere. Even elite athletes were saying that their sponsorship was dying off and they were only getting 20 per cent of what they needed. This was worldwide.

Then on 22 February a magnitude 6.3 earthquake rocked Christchurch. Buildings tottered, suburbs were swamped with liquefaction, the cathedral fell, the Canterbury TV building collapsed and caught fire, cars and buses were crushed and masonry and glass rained down on people. In the end, 185 people lost their lives. The quake resulted in tens of billions of dollars of damage. It made raising money for a bike race seem trivial and mean. People came out with the line that 'life goes on', that I shouldn't feel bad about it – but I did. Fundraising slowed right down.

I don't like asking for funding in the first place. I'm the sort of person who can go out and ask for support for someone else, but for myself . . .

Michelle did proposals for me and lined up companies. Other people lined up companies for me, too, but I then had to 'sell' myself in these encounters. In my mind, I wondered why it wasn't good enough that I beat everyone on a bike. But they want to see the person who's going to promote their organisation or product. Michelle came with me on one of these coffee meetings, and I was sitting there fiddling my fingers and not really engaging with the guy.

What I found was that this was just another skill I needed to learn, something that you can train for. I've now given lots of talks on my riding and training – but it's something else I'll need to put mileage into.

All of these things were going on and I was trying to train. And work. I was down to three- and four-day weeks and I was on wages, so money was getting tight. There was nothing extra floating around. And while I was driving around in my van, working, all I could think about was the race, the crew and the stress. Then I would have to put in hours of training at night, and I was already feeling like mud.

Then two weeks before the departure date for California, Robyn, the crew chief, pulled out.

This was the hardest part of the whole build-up. Robyn and Phil had been really good friends of mine, especially after the break-up with Dianna. I remembered saying to Phil a long time before this happened that I was possibly going to lose a few friends through doing the RAAM. He reminded me of that later, after I got back from the US, and he asked me, 'Was it worth it?' And I said, 'Yeah, it was.' I was prepared for that to happen.

From my point of view, I saw this last crew withdrawal as a clash of personalities between Robyn and Michelle. There was a major rift between them. Both are very strong-minded. Some people don't know how to take Michelle. She is very much straight to the point – some people struggle to deal with that and some people don't.

To a degree, I was sheltered from these conflicts, even though they inhabited my mind. I was on my bike, training, cranking through the k's. My fight, I felt, was on the road, in the saddle of my bike, bending my back into the training. I didn't need this side-tracking. I needed focus. I just wanted to block everything out. And that's what I was probably guilty of most. It could possibly have been sorted out much earlier.

Part of the conflict between Robyn and Michelle stemmed from Michelle stepping in and doing things for me. Robyn was setting tasks like organising logistics and crew details, and I felt I had enough to do with work and training, but I had agreed to do them. A lot of this stuff was unfamiliar to me and I put it off. When Michelle saw that I wasn't following up, she started taking on some of my role as well as her own. I think that Robyn felt she wasn't kept informed of this and perceived it as 'going under the radar'. But it was as a result of procrastination by me, due mostly to the stress of situation. I would start things then not finish them. I was grateful when Michelle helped out with this.

In the end, Michelle was doing the whole lot – making campervan bookings in the States, answering emails, checking on my medical requirements, organising insurance. This all took a toll on our new relationship. We look back now and it was quite a harsh beginning.

Another point of tension developed over back-up crew. As soon as Mike raised all the sponsorship issues, it was clear that he was dissatisfied with the set-up and signalled that he might pull out. Michelle could see that there was potential for derailing the campaign if we didn't have the personnel, so she organised back-up crew – in this case, a back-up mechanic. Michelle's concern was that we needed to avoid any potential problems that might arise once we got overseas. If crew bailed on us at that point, there would be no way to recover.

One of the things I needed to sort out was the kinds of medication I should take on the RAAM. The pain starts after a few hours of an enduro event, and persists for the rest of the event, moving from one muscle, joint or tendon to another. For the qualifier around Lake Taupo, I'd had a huge concoction of drugs. I got quite sick in the stomach. We organised a sports doctor and Michelle, Robyn and I visited him together. It turned out that I was just taking too much. All I required were two types of drugs – an anti-inflammatory and a painkiller. And I was to take these only when I needed them. The strategy was to hold out until it was absolutely necessary that I have them, then only take them as prescribed. This worked out a lot better than Taupo.

Prior to this doctor's visit, Robyn had written an extensive email, eventually asking if Michelle wanted to be the crew chief. The problem was one of communication. Michelle hadn't been letting her know what she had been doing on my behalf. But to Michelle and me, this wasn't a problem. She was doing the things that I couldn't – or wouldn't – do.

We met Robyn in a café after the visit to the doctor. It was an awkward gathering. We talked about the tensions that had developed in the team – this was becoming painful for all three of us. Michelle thought that Robyn was being defensive. Robyn then concluded things saying, 'I'm not doing this.' She left. I was horrified, dumbstruck. I just didn't know what to say. I certainly didn't know how to repair things.

Could I have stopped the blow-up? Maybe. Perhaps it was going to happen anyway. If we had established the differences earlier and discussed them, if that had happened, then we could have dealt with it sooner. But that's the perfect view of hindsight.

When Robyn pulled out, we just had to pick up straight away. There were just two weeks left until departure.

Michelle stepped into the breach. She had lived and breathed the build-up to the race, my qualifying in the Taupo race, buying the gear, planning the diet, the medical needs, checking on the myriad requirements as stipulated by the race administrators. She also had a quality that I'd later find out was all-important in a crew chief – grit and determination. She had the ability to make tough calls – and to be tough at crucial moments. This advice was given in the RAAM handbook. The crew chief was to be in charge, absolutely.

You read books about the RAAM and the notes from the RAAM manual and they all stress that you should have a crew chief and that that person should hold the reins. There's no guessing or second-guessing – that person calls the shots.

Michelle took that role on and did really well. It is always the most disliked job, the one where a person makes the decisions.

Gavin McCarthy from V.I.C. Cycles became my mechanic for the race, once it became clear that Mike wouldn't make it.

My old mate Dion McKenzie and his partner, Georgina 'George' Nation, took the places that Shane and Greg had left open and I was glad to have them on board.

Dion had been a friend of mine from Monrad Intermediate in Palmerston North. After that, we'd gone to different colleges and lost contact. Then we'd come across each other again during one of the Moonride mountain-bike races and it was like we'd just said goodbye yesterday. I instantly felt completely at ease and natural with him. There are few people in your life that you have that sort of immediate and natural affinity with.

What was good about Dion and George was that they could just muck in, adapt. They're typical, relaxed Kiwi travellers. It wouldn't be a problem if they hadn't showered for five days, or the sleeping arrangements weren't perfect, or meals were irregular. And that's what you need for a RAAM team: people who are flexible, robust, who can roll with the inevitable changes.

I don't think I would have made it to the RAAM without Michelle. She was the one who finally convinced me that I could get there. She persuaded me, too, that I needed specialised coaching. I wouldn't have gone with Silas, otherwise, and got the particular, targeted programme that he developed. I knew, eventually, that I could ride it, but I didn't think I could afford it, or organise it, but she actually made me think that I could. She was the one that set things in motion and who insisted that I actually had to put the pieces in place to make it happen. She was also looking at things long term, and saying, 'You could hit an obstacle there.' That's quite a valuable attribute. But those people who pulled out – Robyn, Phil, Mike, Greg, Shane – all contributed hugely, with fund-raising, organisation, equipment and friendship, for which I will always be tremendously grateful.

Things mend. People knew how much the RAAM meant to me and how much I'd sacrificed to get up to that stage, to make it to that race.

Mike and I are still friends. He still sponsors me. Our relationship is a little different, but it's good. It's more professional now. The one thing I know about Mike, that I'm certain about, is that he really cares about me, really cares about my result, when I'm racing. You can't ask for more.

Chapter 7

Californian heat

The jet touched down at Los Angeles International Airport late in the afternoon. The flight from the Southern Hemisphere winter to the Californian heat of the Northern Hemisphere had taken a civilised 12 hours. I travel really well when flying long distance – I take a knockout drop and sleep the whole way.

Gavin McCarthy, the crew mechanic, had been waiting for us in the bustle of the LAX terminal for six hours, having arrived on an earlier flight. He was toting a diary his girlfriend, Rebecca 'Becks' Houston had made for him. This was a lovely book, with flags of each state we'd pass through and visitor highlights of places we'd stay at before and after the race. Becks had further decorated these pages with her own detailed line drawings and patterns. Gavin would write in this during our stay in America. It was a way for them to be close for the month they would be apart.

A little lanky, as you would expect a road cyclist to be, Gavin is good-natured and an easy presence to be around. You could tell straight away that there would be no dramas around him on the road. His own passion was for mountain biking.

We picked up the rental vehicle, a Dodge people mover that would act as the follow vehicle for the race, loaded the gear and we were on our way. The road bike, training bike and time-trial bike were being brought over on two separate flights to spread the risk of damage and loss. We had brought over the time-trial bike and road bike. Dion and George were bringing over the race bike.

Michelle drove. I just wanted to sightsee, soak up the place. Los Angeles was all the movie clichés I'd seen and so much more. We passed palm trees, a Goodyear blimp, then into our first experience of a six-lane highway. In the race to come, I would be riding down a few of these multi-lane monsters – well, three-lane freeways.

The race route mainly followed back roads, away from heavy traffic. Safety was a consideration that the RAAM organisers took extremely seriously, and this was always the first item on the agenda. But it was impossible to avoid these multi-lane arteries on occasions, and travelling at 25 kilometres per hour while massive cars rocketed by at 110 kilometres per hour felt like playing Russian roulette with more than one bullet in the gun. This is when your support team's nerve, skill and courage keep you alive.

The drive from the airport was down the coast toward San Diego, which is about another hour's drive beyond Oceanside. There seemed to be one beach town after another, like huge suburbs sprawling out from LA.

Oceanside, where the RAAM was to start from, is a smallish city with a good surf beach. Marine Corps Base Camp Pendleton is also there, however, so there is a military mix with the laid-back Californian atmosphere. You could go and get a full army kit in the six or seven army surplus stores in the centre of the city, all selling the same stuff. Then there was the Mexican flavour, quite literally, with Mexican restaurants and stands selling tacos and tamales. Oceanside had the usual lines of palms, Spanish-style beachfront hotels, white-sand beaches crowded with swimmers, surfers and sunbathers.

We checked in at La Quinta Inn, a motel back from the beach with off-street parking. This was an ideal spot to assemble the bikes and kit out the vehicles. Then we explored Oceanside on foot. The temperature was in the early twenties, like a good New Zealand summer – shorts and T-shirt weather – even though a shore breeze came in from the ocean. We spotted a surf museum that Gavin and Michelle were keen on visiting and then wandered along the pier, a major attraction. This is a wide wooden structure nearly 600 metres long. A local institution on the pier is Ruby's Diner. It was a diner with a 1950s vibe, with waitresses dressed like they just walked out of *American Graffiti*. They served great burgers, chips – oops, fries – and milkshakes in tall scalloped glasses. I could get used to this.

◌⚲◌

I was there for the ultimate test. Only a few people knew that. I walked around the beach community as anonymous as the next person. It was strange that the surfers and the beach bunnies were hanging out and having light-hearted fun as I went into the final phase of the race build-up. Not to say there isn't a biking community there. In fact, cycling's quite big on the coast, but the RAAM has little profile. It's a bit like comparing people who have been on a domestic flight to those who have flown to the moon. Except that going to the moon makes you famous, and doing the RAAM puts you on the extreme fringe of the sporting community – any further out and you'd be getting a visit from men in white coats to fit you out with a special jacket.

The RAAM is big in the sense of the actual race, its length and the fortitude needed by a competitor to finish it. But it's a small race in the scale of its publicity and the penetration it has into the popular imagination. The Tour de France is glamorous, fast-paced duelling between riders; the RAAM is a grinding, ragged, lonely battle. Not many people know about it. It's probably got a bigger internet following than people physically witnessing it. And there's nominal TV coverage, unlike two of the earlier races when the RAAM began that had a big network covering them.

While we were in Oceanside, a couple of us went into a shop that had a RAAM poster in the window. The woman tending the shop thought we were from Scotland by our accent and asked what we were doing in California. We told her that we were there to do the RAAM that was starting in Oceanside in a few days. She had no idea what we were talking about.

To date, there's been a couple of hundred solo riders to finish the RAAM since its inception in 1982. Most team riders finish. Only about 50 per cent of the solo riders finish. 4828 kilometres without drafting. You're always pushing against the full pressure of the air pushing back at you, and any headwind seems to multiply that resistance. It's not like bunch riding when there's a big group of bikes. A peloton creates its own slipstream and slices through the air. A solo rider is up against that alone, along with the rest of the elements. There's no hiding in a pack.

A RAAM solo rider pushes hundreds of thousands, if not millions, of pedal strokes during the race. Hundreds of thousands of strokes for each ankle, each Achilles tendon, each calf, thigh and knee. And the glutes and lower back would be processing all that, too. And this within the 12-day timeframe that meant a minimum of over 400 kilometres a day. The fastest riders would clock up a staggering 560 kilometres a day – a killer pace, for sure. The course passed through a desert, accumulated over 51,000 metres of hill climbs and, even though held in summer, regularly ran into a storm or two – and snow.

The Anza-Borrego Desert worried me most. I'd never been in a desert before. Desert heat held a mythical quality and occupied a space in my mind where cowboys rode their horses to exhaustion and the skeletons of longhorn cattle littered the sand. This was in the first part of the race, and accounted for quite a few of the riders who fell by the wayside. I learned later that other riders train in this huge, bare stretch of burnt land, staying there to acclimatise before the event.

Our budget was slim enough to be deemed malnourished – there was no fat for this sort of training luxury. The budget was so lean, in fact, that Gavin was going to stay in a portacot in Michelle's and my motel room. Dion and George were driving the campervan that would act as home and headquarters down from LA, and those two and Max Neumegen, a New Zealand registered nurse who was going to take care of my health needs, would sleep in this on the road prior to the race.

The course changed from year to year, but always pushed off on the North Pacific Coast and ended on the Atlantic Coast. This year, it would start in Oceanside in California and would finish nearly 5000 kilometres later in Annapolis, Maryland, passing through 14 states.

The prospect of being roasted in the desert as a RAAM entrant sprung into my mind.

During our first week in Oceanside, we familiarised ourselves with the place and bought and prepared gear. Gavin built up my time-trial bike and my training bike. And later when my road bike arrived, after it had gone on a detour to Sydney, Australia, only turning up five days before race start, he got it into tip-top shape. We went for rides most days – either the very light, taper-down rides that Silas prescribed – or we'd hire cruiser bikes at the pier and take in the sights.

I'm guessing that Gavin thought that we were cycling in slow motion during the training rides. He took part in a few friendly, local bunch races that set off from Nitro, one of the big bike shops there. Despite being a mountain-bike rider, he took a couple of third places out of fields of 50 and won some sprint sections. It was great having the crew mechanic jousting with the locals – it injected the sort of spirit and energy we needed in the campaign.

We visited several bike shops. One of these had lines of elite European bikes at US $7000-plus apiece, and row upon row of deep-dish carbon wheels.

We also had frequent visits to the frozen yoghurt shop. Gavin would put a multi-coloured variety of syrups, along with M&M's, nuts, fruit and cookies, on his enormous dishes of this frozen delight.

Food was a preoccupation. Anything, from the free breakfast of sausages, bacon and scrambled eggs at the motel, to the burgers in diners, to the Crab Palace, hotdogs and various other fast food stands, even the food from vending machines back at the motel – I was into it.

I saw one barbecue in the street that was about two metres long and one wide. It had a deep grate of glowing charcoal and cuts of meat that must have three to six kilos in weight sizzling irresistibly on it.

I felt ravenous the whole time we were in Oceanside, and the physical pleasure of food was a welcome distraction from the detail of the preparations.

That sort of eating was fine for our stay in Oceanside. But food for the race was quite a different matter. The diet Michelle had devised before we left New Zealand went out the window. The way you got food in the States was so different to New Zealand. Nearly everything was pre-packaged, pre-flavoured and ready to eat. Even food in a delicatessen had been pre-sliced and sealed in plastic vacuum packs. Foods that we took for granted, quite basic stuff – baked beans, say, or a bag of rice – were unobtainable. You couldn't buy the meat, the pasta and vegetables to make a bolognese – this was sold as a pre-made meal. You couldn't be sure of what you were getting or what it would taste like.

Generally, everything seemed a lot sweeter and a lot fattier. California wasn't so bad, but when we went inland, the crew reckoned they couldn't find anything. It became one takeaway after another – one long junk-food run across the States.

And then there were foods I was meant to avoid, those that I was meant to eat before I went to sleep and things I was meant to eat when I woke up. Before I slept I wasn't supposed to eat dairy products, bananas, foods with caffeine, or high carb–low GI foods. This proposed regime fell over. It became a case of just scoff whatever you could eat, whatever you could stomach, whatever you could find.

The crew did buy a lot of fresh fruit and vegetables in the first part of the race, but the fridge in the campervan was small. The produce just went mouldy. They didn't bother much with fresh stuff as the race wore on. There weren't enough people to cook it either. So whenever the crew did have time for someone to cook something, it was heaven.

Dion and George arrived with the campervan seven days before the race, which prompted more shopping trips as we kitted it out. The van held multiple changes of clothes and shoes, bike spares, the crew's gear, food and chilly bins of ice. The follow vehicle held a mini mechanical set-up for emergencies and instant repairs when the campervan wasn't nearby. Max, who was in his early fifties, completed our team. An experienced nurse, he had his own shopping requirements for medical supplies.

Dion, George and Max had the campervan parked on the main street for the free parking, another miserly move on our part to screw the budget down as tight as we could. One hitch with this was that it's illegal to sleep parked in a city street. The idea was that the three would keep a low profile – not an entirely successful strategy, as it turned out. One night, Max was on the computer at about 1am when there was a knock at the window. Instead of checking what it was about, he closed the laptop and hurriedly drew the curtain in a vain attempt to pretend that no one was there. Then there was a hammering on the door. The crew opened it to a very large and extremely pissed-off cop. There was no citation for them using the campervan while parked on the street, but a lengthy tirade for ignoring the law when it came knocking.

Gavin and I checked over the RAAM start. The first 40 kilometres of the course is unsupported, so no one can accompany a rider. We wanted to work out which would be the best bike and wheels for this initial part of the course. Also, I wanted it clear in my mind exactly where to go from the start line. The RAAM route book is a marvel of precision and clarity. It contains every corner and turn for the whole race, distances, brief descriptions of the places you'd pass through, and all the time stations. The time stations, or checkpoints, are places where you need to check in with RAAM headquarters. This reporting tracked progress but was essentially another safety measure from the organisers, ensuring that everything was okay. Missing time station check-ins could result in time penalties.

We rode to this first checkpoint, Lake Henshaw, and back, taking it easy and chatting nearly the whole way. There were a few hills, short five-minute climbs, and the heat built noticeably the further from the coast we travelled. There's nothing at Lake Henshaw, just a lake with a couple of trees around it. And that's it. To me, this was like the desert already – dry, dusty and nothing there, just this forlorn lake holding out against the heat.

The next day I did this again, solo. Michelle and Gavin drove in the support vehicle, meeting me at the first checkpoint. This was our try-out for the start of the race. It went without a hitch. But I could feel the clock ticking, counting down the seconds to race day. Did we have everything we needed? How well prepared were we, really? There were some things we wouldn't know until we got into the race.

One thing that was becoming clear, however, was that we were light on crew. We were one of the first teams to arrive at the motel. Other teams that came in later said that we were going to find it tough with just five. They pointed out that other solo teams had between eight and ten in their crews. These conversations were with team-racing crews and riders in the Race Across the West, a shorter race following the same route, which was also run by RAAM. They'd done these races a few times before. Some of them had done the RAAM, and they were quite helpful with tips. But they were tips I probably didn't need to hear.

I was told by a couple of different guys who had done RAAM before that I shouldn't go too fast at the start. My whole plan was to go out hard and fast. This advice really got in my head. They mentioned it so much that I started to believe it myself. To have a measured, conservative start to keep a store of energy had obviously been their race plan. But they didn't know my ability. I was probably faster than most of those guys, anyway. It was an error in judgement listening to them and taking their well-meant advice on board.

We didn't talk to the other solo guys at our motel, other than to say hello. They were the competition, after all, so there was this mutually invoked silence. Understandable, as you don't want to share your information.

Out on the race itself, you'd get members from other crews who'd approach your crew and say things like, 'You haven't got your hazard lights on.' Or some other perceived infringement. Then you'd actually find that you're not supposed to have them on. They were telling you this with an implied threat that they would contact the race organisers and you might receive a time penalty, a 15-minute addition to your time. But these sorts of interactions only happened close to the start. A few days into the race, and you hardly saw anyone.

We packed the car and campervan in preparation for an inspection. RAAM officials checked that the bikes, wheels, helmets and shoes had the required lights and reflectors. They checked that the signage on the vehicles was in the correct position, first for safety, and second for media coverage. Then there was a RAAM meeting in a community hall down by the pier in which were gathered some winners in the solo division from the first thirty years of the race. Some of these guys were quite old by then, a reminder that endurance racing favours a few years under your belt before you have the sinewy strength to compete and the leathery resolve to finish.

Then all the solo riders were invited onto the stage. This was the field. The 50 or so driven enough to lay their bodies and minds on the line, to peel away the layers of their vigour and sanity and stare down defeat in the most taxing sporting event of their lives – would they finish the course, or would it finish them?

Chapter 8

A Kiwi in the desert

I botched the start.

Looking back on this, I understand what contributed to the stumble at the start. But it doesn't change the reality. I choked on the occasion, on the seriousness of the event and the enormity of what I had to do. I blew the beginning, and I have to live with that. And I had to deal with that going into the first part of the race.

The start is an opportunity to establish an opening advantage. I could go fast at the beginning, with freshness and force. It would be the only time during the race that I could go this hard for such a sustained period of time. It's natural to rip into a race from the outset, to burn through the adrenaline and pent-up energy. This was the race plan. The idea had been to just lock into the pedals, get my legs pumping and go. And once through that opening burst, a day or so down the track, I would settle into the hard, relentless rhythm of the race. But I didn't – I got riled up in the event, I gave way to nerves.

There were a few factors that fed into this. The other riders I'd met at the Oceanside hotel had warned me against starting too fast. Conserve your energy. Keep your eye on surviving the long haul. Leave some gas in your tank. That was the advice. Wrong, wrong, wrong.

After talking with them, I was infected with doubt. Doubt is like a virus for a sportsperson. It infects every cell in your body. It's debilitating, draining on your mental energy, and damaging to your focus. And in all sports, you win the race in your mind. You work on mental toughness as much as you work on pushing pedals around. It's the wheels spinning in your head that keep the wheels spinning beneath your body. I was infected with doubt – and suddenly very nervous.

The race day came. The start was at lunchtime. The crew had packed everything away. Gavin had my road bike in slick condition. I was jittery.

We'd seen the starts of other divisions on the previous day. Women riders start the race a day before men. And after this, the over-60 men. The riders started the race with an announcement, who they were, their country of origin and a brief bio of their significant races. This would be the format the next day for the solo guys. At the pre-race briefing you're given your individual race number and starting time. Each racer will be pulsed out a minute apart. The number you're allocated is unique. Once you've entered the race, it is your number for life.

The start is low-key, held in a carpark at Oceanside Pier.

I sat on my bike and Michelle and the crew milled around. You can't help but look about and check out the other riders and their set-ups. There were some big crews – ten plus – with flash vehicles. Very professional looking and well practised. Experience and confidence shone from these outfits. The majority of the field were US and European riders. Here we were with this tiny crew from down under. We hardly had any experience with this sort of racing. And we were up against seasoned and well-financed veterans of endurance racing.

All the effort to get there came back to me, the begging and borrowing, making it on the thinnest shoestring of a budget. All the training and preparation, the coaching and support, the long night rides, early mornings at the gym – the sweat and determination. All that came to this point. I was there at the start line and I didn't feel too confident.

The riders, one by one, went up onto a small ramp, like a time-trial ramp. This elevated them so they could be seen by the crowd. As they sat on their bikes, a race organiser introduced the rider to the crowd then read out all the races they'd done. Some of these resumés were extraordinarily impressive. There were Olympians and national champions.

The longest race I would have done before this mind-blowing epic was a trifling 1280 kilometres, and here I was, in the peak event of endurance cycle racing. A lot of the riders had done the RAAM before. Even many of the rookie solo entrants had done the RAAM as part of two-, four- or eight-member teams. All the rookies like me had the highest numbers. Mine is 414. The old hands had lower numbers — they started last.

My time came. I walked my bike up the ramp and mounted it. The race official introduced me and read a list of my racing feats. Before I pushed off, he quietly said to me, 'I hope you made love to your sweet lady last night because you won't be doing that for a while.' It was a kind and tension-breaking thing to say. He obviously saw that I was as nervous as hell.

Then I was on my way. In the last few races in New Zealand I was the favourite to win from the start. But this wasn't New Zealand and it wasn't a Taupo enduro. At the beginning of the race, I only had to do a U-turn, go along the beach onto the next terrace, then turn a corner. I'd completely forgotten which corner.

I'd practised this start several times beforehand but I went down the wrong street. I came back, majorly flustered. And yet, a few days earlier, I had done that whole start. I'd done all the turns and pedalled up through the California hills . . . And just a small thing like that really threw me.

Michelle later said that she'd never seen me so nervous. As the new crew chief, she became worried about how I would perform. How would she get me out of this cloud of anxiety? She was the person closest to me, as a partner and crew chief.

It was really just the occasion. I'd let it get to me. I'd let the other riders tell me about going off too fast. I shouldn't have listened. We had our race plan. I was meant to go off quite fast. Then the heat affected me. And this was before I'd even hit the desert.

The first 13 kilometres are known as the 'parade zone'. You're not allowed to pass anyone until you reach a bridge that signals the end of this phase of the race. I eventually found my way out of Oceanside and there was a big bunch of us cycling along by this dry riverbed, parched and dusty as the inside of my throat and mouth. And as soon as we got to the bridge everyone went for it.

Riders with lower numbers flew past me – RAAM veterans bent to their handlebars kicked into the first part of the race, asserting their skill and knowledge with each pedal stroke. 'I know what I'm doing,' their momentum seemed to say, 'do you?'

Support vehicles weren't allowed to meet up with riders till the first checkpoint, Lake Henshaw. After this, leapfrog support was allowed. This meant the support vehicle could drive ahead, then stop on the side of the road until the racer caught up, and after they'd passed the vehicle could 'leapfrog' again. The reason for this was so that there weren't all these slow vehicles bunched on the road. This safety rule lasted through the first few States.

I felt overheated and couldn't get my liquid food down. I was nauseous and overwrought, with a whole combination of things attacking me at once. My pace dropped off. And I was worried about the desert. The heat was already shrivelling me. At the same time, the idea of the desert was tantalising. I thought, 'What's the desert going to be like?' Then I thought, 'Shit, what *is* the desert going to be like?'

The ride out of Oceanside and toward the Anza-Borrego Desert takes you up through the California hills. You climb 1200 metres through brown and golden rolling country dotted with sage-green bushes. These were short climbs, but there was a succession of them, rising up and up over these humps of dried grasses.

At the top, there's this astonishing view. The road winds down and around the hills on the other side. This is called the glass elevator. As this road twists and switches back on itself there are these panoramas of the desert from different angles.

Seeing the desert for the first time, I was amazed at its scale. It's huge. An enormous basin smothered in rippling waves, glistening with heat. I couldn't see the end of it. I suddenly realised how huge this country was. And I was about to ride across it. It struck me, too, that I wouldn't be near the sea until the end of the ride. In New Zealand the coast is only ever an hour's drive away. From one coastline to the other, crossing the country width-wise, was easily cycle-able in a day.

As I descended, there was a man on the side of the road that I took to be a RAAM race official. He was raising and lowering his hand: Slow down! I did so. Then I went on a bit further and I realised why I'd received the warning. On the side of the road was a race bike with its forks buckled in. There had been a bad crash. There was a woman covered in blood next to the bike. She didn't appear to be injured, so

I assumed she was a member of the crew. I took this all in with the glimpse that I got as I shot past.

I've seen plenty of bike crashes and been involved in a few myself. If you're doing a race like this, you've got to be prepared that that may happen. It wasn't great seeing this, but it was a part of what could happen, albeit an unappealing part. It's a hard surface to hit.

I took a measured approach down the glass elevator from there. The elevator dropped the 1200 metres I'd climbed, and then some, taking me to below sea level.

The lower down toward this basin I went, the higher the heat rose. But then there was a sudden spike. I went around a corner, dropped down and the oven door opened. A fiery wave hit me. It was like passing through an invisible wall – on one side was hot air, on the other a hostile, ferocious heat.

This was late afternoon, between four and five, and it was a roasting 43 degrees. As I was told later, Max genially pointed out to the crew that we hit the desert at the best time. The rise from unbearable to intolerable temperatures during the day had a definite span, and it was best not to be in the desert between 11am and 2pm. Midday was the worst. Late afternoon onwards and toward night was preferable.

Before I went to the RAAM, because it was the beginning of winter in New Zealand and was getting cold, I thought I needed heat training. So when I was at the gym, I'd sit in the sauna for a while. This was a bit ad hoc, but better than nothing. When the sauna got up to the late 30s, I thought it was getting a little too hot to handle. When it got over 40 a couple of times, it was practically unbearable.

But the desert was different. It was a dry heat and I was moving. There was a little bit of air moving over me but I could still feel the heat coming up off the road onto my legs. The road through the desert is made out of huge slabs of concrete. This reflected the light like a heater pointed upward. At night, this concrete would be like a big storage heater, releasing the heat it had absorbed during the day.

It was stifling. The crew stopped at the side of the road to wait for me and they couldn't believe how baking hot it was.

I pedalled into this. Cadence is all I had. I moved my legs around. I was in the desert. The heat dispelled any doubt of that. It swallowed you and you moved through it on its terms.

It was so hot, in fact, that I didn't sweat. The moisture would dry on my skin as it came out of my pores, leaving just a mineral deposit on my skin. I didn't experience the feeling of sweat on me for the whole desert.

I'd listened to bad advice – for me, at least – to hold back. But one tip that I'd picked up from other riders was on the button. And, I'm sure for some, lifesaving. You can't drink enough liquid going through the desert. Even if you think you're drinking too much, you're not drinking enough.

I was constantly drinking as I rode along. I'd gone away from the food altogether and drank electrolytes. I ate what I could, but the main thing for me through the desert was to keep up the fluids. Dehydration is what lands most people in hospital in this area. We were so scared of it that the crew made sure I was drinking the whole time. You can, of course, over-hydrate. But there was no danger of that there.

We'd brought the time-trial bike for long flat stretches of road – like the desert. That was the plan. A time-trial bike is a bit heavier at the front and is more highly geared than a race bike. Riding it, you lean forward into a more stream-lined position. This is what I was meant to ride, but my race bike was comfortable. The light, carbon-fibre race bike was what I had ridden so often that it felt like a part of me. I didn't want to change from it.

In hindsight, the crew should have got me onto the time-trial bike. They should have forced me to ride it and pointed out that we shouldn't change the race plan. Not yet. Not after 12 hours into the race. This was something that the crew learned and something that I learned. At the end of the day, I've just got to do what I'm told. My race plan should be set out before we start. That's it. Of course, the crew needs to be responsive to what's happening with me. But they tell me what to do – I don't tell them.

The plan had been to go hard from the outset, perhaps for 30 or 40 hours. To just race for that distance, then start the grind. That's how the race is run. All the top guys abso-lutely nail it from the start, then everyone gets down to their endurance pace and rolls along the countryside at that pace. After that, the idea is to keep moving. You're not going to get to the finish line if you stop. You've got to keep the forward momentum going. And that's the trick of the crew the whole time – to keep the rider moving, in all circumstances. The winner takes the race in the first 40 hours, as long as they can keep up their endurance pace and stay awake.

Sunburn was the next thing to address. A red-headed, fair-skinned Kiwi coming out of a New Zealand winter and into the desert was a recipe for roast lobster. The crew was constantly slathering ridiculous amounts of sunscreen onto me.

About a month after Michelle and I got back from the United States, I went skiing for the first time. We took the sunscreen we'd used on the RAAM and I was meant to put it on my face, but I couldn't. I'd had so much of it caked on my face over the race. Just the smell – I couldn't stand it. I nearly vomited from the thick odour wafting out of the container. But it was the most effective brand for me, so it's difficult to change.

I knew that I was going a bit slower than I had originally hoped, but the goal at this time was to survive the desert. In the back of my head I was concerned about losing position. I was conscious of maintaining what pace I had, of keeping on going, of just moving ahead. This was a race, and the competitive heart still beat in my body, but there was another competition here, the fight with the desert.

I had settled into a rhythm. I was coping. Every so often a crew member – Dion, George, Gavin – would wait by the side of the road and squirt a shower of icy water onto me. This refreshing rain cut through the heat and washed off the salt that had dried on my skin. Perhaps because I struggled with the heat so much climbing into the desert, and I was so worried about the heat I'd experience once I descended again, actually dealing with it was a relief. It was still energy sapping. I pushed on.

One of the surprising things about dropping into the desert, into this scorching, merciless heat, is that one of

Pre-race organisation of food and drink supplies in Oceanside, California, June 2011.

Receiving our race brief and solo rider introductions in Oceanside, two days prior to the start of the RAAM.

Looking down on the team vehicles alongside Oceanside Beach on race day, June 2011.

Proud Kiwis before the start of the RAAM. Left to right: George, Dion, Michelle, me, Max and Gavin.

Being interviewed on the start ramp.

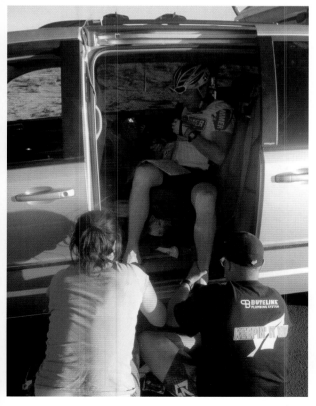

George and Dion changing my socks while I rummage for food.

Entering the Anza-Borrego Desert, California, in 40+ degree heat.

Monument Valley, Arizona.

Riding past my follow vehicle during a leap-frog section of the race.

Dion up to his usual
tricks, trying to keep
me entertained.

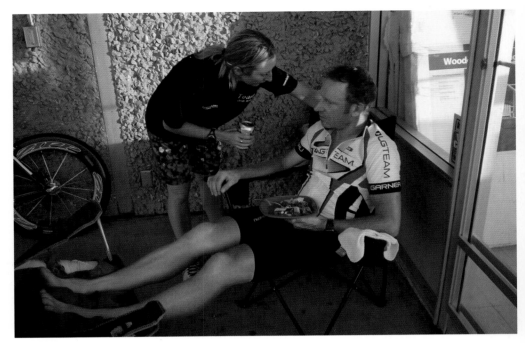

A typical pose for me—feet up with a plate of food, with Michelle
handing me a root beer.

Crossing the border into Utah.

Cycling up Wolf Creek Pass, Colorado.

Time station 32 in Camdenton, Missouri, where I had McDonald's and KFC.

Keeping up with the locals in Indiana.

Crossing the finish line in Annapolis, Maryland, 10 days, 5 hours and 27 minutes after leaving Oceanside.

the first things you ride up to is a massive casino. It had the biggest carpark I'd ever seen, bigger than any carpark even for the largest New Zealand mall.

We had been warned by the police before the start about drunk drivers in the desert. This seemed unlikely. Drunks in the desert? How could that be possible? Were there saloons out there? Then we saw the casino. Liquored-up gamblers could be rolling out of that place at any time of the day or night. We didn't, however, encounter any drunken driving. There wasn't much traffic at all.

I passed a large sign that announced an Indian reservation. But that's all there was, nothing else. Presumably there was a settlement somewhere, but it wasn't visible from the highway.

It didn't seem to cool that much with nightfall, but the temperature did drop a little. It was like biking on a really hot summer's day in New Zealand, but this was night. The moon rose. It was an extraordinary sight – a big shining moon lighting up the sand dunes and the straggly shrubs and grasses. Everything was golden and dusty with these bright green cactuses poking up. The dunes looked like golden waves – they seemed to go on forever. And there was this weird effect – the sand dunes seemed to move.

With the luminosity of the moon, I hardly needed any lights to see where I was going. Then there was this movement on the road. It was this fine, dusty sand. It must have been the lightest puff of a breeze moving this sand as there was no wind, none that I could detect. This shifted like a thin veil across the road and over the dunes. I'd see the road in front of me and the whole thing would sort of shimmer and move sideways. But then the road was exactly where it had been. It was this thin film that had drifted across it.

It was cool to watch but it made cycling odd. I didn't know what this stuff was doing. Was it going to blow over me? The sand was so fine it was like a veil waving over the road. Every now and then it went swish, right across both lanes and I'd have to adjust my sense of reality again.

I quite like riding at night. And even in this heat, I found myself admiring the effects the night brought to this stark landscape. I was over the start and had settled down. I had got back into the race, and the idea that I was going to be doing this for the oncoming days. I started thinking about catching people. I'd been passed by a few people at the start and they came into my thoughts. My competitiveness was rising, it was cooler and the food was going down a little better, and the excitement of being in the race returned. I was in this new place, a desert, with this drift sand flitting in front of me. The moon traversed the sky like a night-time sun.

With the dawn, the bare emptiness stretched out before me once more. The same ragged bushes and cactuses, a rickety, ancient fence, and the same parched emptiness on either side of the long straight road. And it was hot. The crew was keeping me well supplied with drinks. I needed them. This was the main desert ride. There was a small headwind and the heat was ferocious and building.

I suffered this out through to past the middle of the day, then came to the climb that would take me from below sea level and up to 334 metres and out of the desert. I was going to do this in the hottest part of the day. It was stinking hot.

We stopped just before the climb. One of the pieces of advice from the RAAM organisers is to make sure you have plenty of ice and replenish it regularly. We had chilly bins in both the campervan and the follow vehicle. And we had an ice vest. This is a vest that is soaked in icy water, then put on. It was a startling sensation, like putting on a coat of snow. I was cool for a while.

As soon as I started climbing the hill, the energy output climbed as well. There's no easy way to summit a hill on a bicycle. That was a long climb in searing sun. I reminded myself that everyone was being punished by the heat. There were still a few riders around, and I could see the stress from the desert temperatures on their faces.

Even after that big climb, I felt like we were still in the desert. It was still hot and barren looking.

This part of the race went to a town called Blythe on the outskirts of California. After the big climb, the country drops down again to about 100 metres above sea level. This is still a really low altitude.

From Blythe I followed the border around to Arizona, and I was climbing again. From there onward, the hills and climbing were constant through two states until the really big ascent into the Colorado Rockies.

I was pretty rapt, because I'd survived the desert. That's where so many riders pull out, get hospitalised with dehydration, heatstroke and related maladies. I knew that, mentally, for me, if I could survive the desert, I was going to finish the race.

Chapter 9

Hotfooting it to Utah

Everybody had bleeding noses. The desert air dried out the crew's sinuses as well as my own.

When I stopped to change my socks, I would sit on the back seat of the follow vehicle and Dion would carefully take my shoes and socks off. He had a wad of tissue jammed up a nostril to staunch the blood. I was tempted to tell him that it improved his looks, but he was being very gentle wiping my feet so I kept quiet.

Like a lot of cyclists, I get 'hot foot'. This is a burning, pins-and-needles sensation in the ball of the foot. It is very unpleasant and for some long-distance cyclists it can be debilitating. It's caused by the 'heads' of the long metatarsal bones squeezing the nerves that pass by them and into the toes. And this squeezing is caused by the pressure of pushing down on the pedal and the feet swelling up.

I'd already changed my shoes to the next size up to accommodate my swollen pups. My right foot is size 45 and my left foot is 46, so I usually wear 46s. I was now wearing 47s – my feet had puffed with the heat not long after the start. We had spare shoes from which we could cut the sides so my feet would have even more room, if needed. Fortunately, we didn't have to do this.

After the PBP and my big Taupo race, we'd also anticipated the possibility of tendonitis in my Achilles. So we also had road shoes on which we could place the cleats further back. The idea was to relieve the pain by shifting the pressure away from the tendon. Once you change something in your position on the bike, however, this has a flow-on effect to other areas of the set-up.

Silas had come up with this solution and had given us a detailed table with adjustments in millimetres for the possibility of tendonitis, but also for other eventualities. Changing the set-up changes the pedal stroke and angles of attack of different muscles and joints. This table of fine adjustments was about protecting my Achilles and my lower back and knees. My knees had blown up already, too. But this wasn't unusual for me and they weren't painful. Yet.

I had regular rub-downs from the crew with Voltaren cream on my calves and quads, the big thigh muscles, and the hamstrings, the muscles up the back of the legs. These were very sore – a massage would have been too painful, but a light rub restored the muscles a little. And the cream helped with the pain . . .

When you hit the 24-hour mark, you can guarantee that things will start hurting, whether it's your back, your knees, your ankles. Just everything starts. For me, it goes in stages. Something will be sore for half a day, then that will go away and something else will take over for a few hours. There's always something that will irritate you. It's a cumulative amount of pain, with your mind withdrawing from one area of discomfort and concentrating on a new area. Something is always sore – the ride is never pain free. When something's giving you grief, it's either going to go numb and stop hurting or something else is going to start hurting. Even your hands get sore, and your forearms and shoulders.

As for my lower back, it just hurt. I knew it was going to hurt. It would hurt, off and on, from start to finish. I would change position on the bike a little and it would go numb, then after a while, the pain would come back.

There was also a spot in my back, between my shoulder-blades, that would go numb. Nearly everything else was sore, but this was just dead.

Then, of course, there was my butt. Before the race, the RAAM organisers gave teams these pamphlets. In them there's a photo of a guy's rear-end, raw all the way up to his back. And I thought, 'Is my bottom going to be like that?' After the first day, I was feeling the wear already.

Max Neumegen saved my butt. Literally. As the crew nurse, he was invaluable. In his mid-fifties, he's a New Zealand registered nurse who specialised in trauma, and was an outdoor first-aid instructor for the New Zealand Mountain Safety Council. He had also been a cyclist in his youth, winning a national title in 1972 as a 16-year-old.

I met him at the Taupo Cycle Challenge Enduro breakfast, which he attended after supporting another cyclist.

A seasoned traveller, he left the country around the same time as us, paid his own way, and was in Los Angeles before the race started. He was keen to be involved with the RAAM. This was perfect.

An inquisitive fellow, before we started out he wondered how we were going to do 24-hour cycling. How was the routine going to work out? He couldn't visualise how we would do this with only five people, two vehicles – one a huge campervan – driving on the opposite side of the road to what we were used to, holding up traffic and following a cyclist. We didn't necessarily have a good answer for this – we weren't too certain ourselves.

Max had all sorts of helpful knowledge related to the expedition. For my backside, he'd organised three potions. I was going to be on my bottom for 24 hours a day for 10 to 12 days. Skin is not made for this. We had a discussion and he decided to use a mixture of creams that would moisten the skin, create a barrier and keep it clean. This would be regularly layered on. And it worked for the entire race.

We also had different seats and seat covers – and lots of different pairs of pants in various brands. The padding in these was different. What had been really good for me in the past couldn't be relied on to be good again. In the end, I didn't wear my flash, expensive pants very much. It was the cheaper pairs that I favoured.

The other thing that Max introduced to me and the crew was glycerine and its marvellous medical properties. This clear, oily liquid is a by-product of manufacturing soap. It has many uses – mainly in food and beauty products. One of glycerine's properties is that it attracts moisture.

Max had come across it in hospitals where it was used to moisten the mouths of elderly people after they'd had an operation. He'd also encountered it in cycling.

An old friend of his would mix one teaspoon of glycerine, a pinch of salt and a teaspoon of glucose to a bottle of water.

We added glycerine to my electrolyte drinks. Hammer and its sub-brands of Head and Fizz were among my sponsors, and I used these electrolyte powders during the race. When the glycerine was mixed with these it made a sort of thicker solution that kept my throat soothed and moist – this was especially good for the arid conditions of the desert. And you could put it up your nose. We did, and the nosebleeds tapered off.

The crew told me the glycerine was good for their throats too. They did a lot of shouting, both in encouragement and hollering directions from the follow vehicle. The microphone and ear buds I used got annoying at times. I'd just pull it out of my ear and stick it in my pocket. So the crew would toot the horn and yell out the window such things as, 'Turn right here!'

After the Taupo qualifier, and the concoction of drugs I'd taken in that race, we were pursuing a more conservative approach with the RAAM. The sports doctor had recommended anti-inflammatories and paracetamol as a standard analgesic. That's it. And not until I needed them – I was to suck it up until then. This worked out really well. The net effect was that my stomach was way more settled. I could get food down more easily – essential when you're outputting so much energy.

The other thing that affects at least one solo rider during the course of each RAAM is Sherma's Neck. With this condition, the neck muscles give out and the sufferer's head falls forward – they can't keep it upright. We had a homemade contraption to deal with this. Gavin's father, Wayne McCarthy, had spent some time making this. It was an ingenious device improvised out of green plastic garden stakes and other 'found' materials. If needed, it would go down my back, parallel to my spine, with a strap that would wrap around my forehead.

Changing socks seemed to be the one thing that relieved the hot foot. And only merino wool socks would do. Not cotton, not cotton mix, but lovely, warm merino socks. Even in the desert heat, these were the ones that worked. I only had three pairs of merino socks and I was changing them every four to six hours.

Something to be aware of in such a long event is the behaviour that begins to undermine your effort. That doubt that I'd had at the start that caused me to deviate from the race plan or, at least, become overwhelmed by the event – that was one of the mental challenges that had to be dealt with. And then there were more insidious behaviours. Like changing socks.

The hot foot was real enough. But when I knew that changing socks meant that I'd stop and I could get off my bike and rest, this became locked in place in my mind. It became immovable and was an impediment to my progress.

When this became more apparent, Michelle tried to push me through it, but I wouldn't budge. I had to change my socks and that was that. These sorts of things need to be picked up on at the start – scrutinised and closely assessed for their effect.

It's a fine line. Perhaps because I was going a little bit slow starting out, I might've been less affected by the desert than if I'd blown a boiler and pushed really hard. You need to be able to recover. You can pick up your rate, but what's that going to do to you two days down the track when you've already taxed your body to a certain extent, and if you go beyond its ability repair itself? I know this is a contradiction – I should've gone faster at the start, for sure. The question is, 'How much faster?'

Michelle said at the end of the race that she never wanted to wash another pair of socks. The campervan was moving along and she – or whoever was on this duty – had to stand up to hand-wash the socks in the sink. These would be hung up on a little line in the back of the van. Towels on the floor beneath them would catch the drips. In fact, nearly everything was done on the move – dishes, cooking, washing or whatever.

I was only dimly aware of these things, of course. My focus was on the road, pedalling.

The first part of Arizona was unremarkable. It seemed like a poor area. The towns were old and run-down looking. The road was bad. And on the side of the road was just more desert-like country. We went through some ugly industrial areas, and straight through the town of Parker – it was quite a big place for where it was located. I may have got this impression of a depressed area because the RAAM route went through back roads. This was to avoid places with high traffic flows.

After Parker was more of the same – dry desert. There was nothing, just the odd little township. The dusty-looking pale sand turned into dusty-looking red dirt.

The whole time, after I'd come out of the desert in California, I was climbing. From Arizona, all way the way to Colorado, starting near sea level, it's constant climbing, then dipping down again, and then more climbing till it reaches close to 3000 metres on the Colorado Plateau. I'd gone over the route book a fair bit before we started. I knew that it was going to be hills all the way to Kansas, that Kansas was going to be flat, then it would get hilly again at the end.

The land changed colour, but it all looked very barren. There was nothing there. That climb – I felt it, it was just at me the whole time. There was no relaxing, no cruising and no free-wheeling. I had to work to keep the bike moving forward. It wasn't an out-of-the-seat grind. It was pressure the whole time – not heavy, but constant.

These were long, straight roads and I couldn't see the end of them. There might be one turn in 100 kilometres. I'd start hanging out for the next corner. I'd ask with the little walkie-talkie I had, 'Have we got a corner coming up soon?' Dion would cheerfully answer, 'Yeah, man, in about 94 kilometres.' These were just straight, featureless roads. When a corner came up, I'd celebrate, Yee-hah! And then there'd be miles of straight road to the next corner . . .

Arizona felt endless. When we first hit the state, I thought, 'Are we only this far through the race?' I knew we'd be in

Arizona for a long time. I'd ask myself, then the crew, 'Are we still in Arizona?' 'Yes,' would come the compassionate reply in my earpiece, 'we're still in Arizona.'

There were various kinds of barrenness in Arizona. We'd go through one flavour of barrenness, then another. Then we'd head into a different set of hills, and then another long straight road. And always on the horizon, in the distance, we could see mountains. These were the Rockies in Colorado.

Every so often there would be something completely random in the middle of the desert. Once we passed this fence, about 20 metres long, with bright yellow horses and 'Chief Yellow Horse' painted on it. There was a big, woven dreamcatcher in front, but nothing else. It was hard to tell if there was anything behind this. There didn't seem to be any horses, and there certainly wasn't any chief around. Then there was another fence with 'Dinosaur tracks, turn now' written on it. But there was nothing there, just desert and a flagpole with half of a ragged American flag flapping in the dry wind.

The checkpoints tended to be around 100 kilometres apart. There were eight in Arizona. That's a big state. We encountered another sort of checkpoint on our way – a government checkpoint searching for illegal immigrants. Presumably these were people who crossed over the border from Mexico. The checkpoint consisted of official vehicles parked diagonally across the road.

The campervan had driven on a couple of hours ahead of me and was waiting with several other RVs involved in the race. There were a couple of border patrol guards checking the documents of people passing through.

Further on, at a RAAM checkpoint in the middle of this empty land, there were marquees set up and a blow-up swimming pool. This was a wonderfully thoughtful thing from the American organisers of that checkpoint. Riders could jump in and cool down. Dion had a splash in it. I didn't. It probably would have been refreshing and would have washed some of that Arizona dust away. But my relationship with swimming water has never been good – even when it's an over-sized paddling pool.

🚲

The leapfrog support continued. This kept the crew fit as they were continually driving up ahead of me, getting my drinks and food ready and, as I passed, they'd run beside me and hand me this stuff. Luckily all this crew were sporty anyway – mountain bikers, cyclists, triathletes.

One thing that I had to get used to was grabbing drinks and food with my left hand when I started getting things from the follow vehicle. Back in New Zealand I would get food from my right, therefore into my right hand. It seems like a small thing, but it was just another instance in which I had to adapt.

On these leapfrog supports Dion pulled the odd stunt to keep up morale. Once I encountered him standing on the side of the road in his underpants, with sunglasses and straw cowboy hat on. He had Gavin's bag at his feet and his thumb out and was holding a sign:

Wellington
New Zealand

At another time, he cartwheeled down the middle of the road beside me saying, 'Look, I'm a tumbleweed, I'm a tumbleweed!'

Dion suggested I change my speedo to one in miles before we went to America. This was a good idea as American distances are in miles, and the RAAM route book, although it had conversions into kilometres, was based on miles. It meant I didn't spend the whole time having to remember that one mile was a little over 1.6 kilometres. The route book itself was incredibly well worked out. The crew had gone through it before the start and had highlighted all the directions for each section, eventually giving up on the GPS as the coverage was unreliable. And sometimes the directions were misleading.

Gavin recalled using the GPS to get to a campground where the campervan toilet could be emptied. George, Dion and Gavin drove for miles through hills carved out of hard red earth. He said the epic expedition was worthwhile because the camping area they eventually came to had a rock formation like humped red hillocks that must have been six storeys high. These had huge cracks running right down them, as if they'd been smacked from above by giant hammer. He showed me the photo later – phenomenal.

The follow car had three people at first: the driver, the navigator and the person prepping my food. This diminished to two people, as the crew got more tired. This shook down as they got the navigation sussed in the end. On the long, straight stretches, crew members sometimes took the opportunity to jump in the back of the follow vehicle and nap. Often the campervan had to take different routes from me, to avoid large vehicles being on – for the US – small roads.

The follow vehicle, then, always had at least two people. One would be driving and the other would be navigating using the route book and doing food prep, mixing drinks and passing food out the window to me.

Michelle said to me later after the race that, as crew chief, she was keeping an eye on how different groupings of people worked out. She would often team up with Max in the follow vehicle, and Max and Dion would work well together. George and Gavin would regularly team up in the follow vehicle also. The other consideration was that Gavin was the main mechanic, but Dion acted as a back-up, so it was a bad strategy to team up Gavin and Dion. It sort of did feel its way out.

She did make a rule in her own mind that the least amount of time any one sub-team could spend in any vehicle was 12 hours. The crew would get tired of being in the follow vehicle and want to be in the campervan. So, she'd put them in the campervan, and pretty much instantly, they'd want to go back in the follow vehicle. This was probably natural – although the scenery was changing all the time, they were in these confined little boxes travelling through this. They were all fit, energetic people, and it was understandable they'd get antsy.

Arizona may have been a long haul through dust, desert and bone-dry air, but the next state, Utah, contained one of the highlights of the entire ride. There was no change going into Utah, it was just the same as Arizona. The route took us only through one corner of Utah, passing from Arizona through a place called Kenyatta and on to Mexican Hat in Utah. This also took us from the Navajo Nation to the Ute people, although the only time any of us met Native American Indians was when Michelle and Dion needed to gas up the RV. They stopped at a souvenir shop that also sold petrol and were served by a man from the local tribe. It was a tired-looking building with a dusty, bare interior. The man was keen for them to buy some trinkets from this rundown place. They didn't – there was no room in the van, and they had very little spare cash. By Michelle's account, he was a warm and friendly chap and they felt sorry they couldn't purchase anything.

Utah was un-spectacular until you hit Monument Valley. This place will forever occupy a monumental place in my mind. Rising above this dry, red-dirt country were these huge, natural sculptures of weathered sandstone.

I hadn't slept for a few days and was getting very fatigued. For a while, I thought these extraordinary formations were man-made, that someone had scaled these and chiselled the features in them. I didn't think this through, obviously. It just seemed inconceivable that such distinct blocks and great cracked towers could have been made with natural processes.

This perception was reinforced by the faces I could see in these massive, upright slabs and skyward pointing fingers. It looked like there were heads carved into these – grand, still, ancient faces. They seemed like alien skyscrapers and pinnacles. They were absolutely amazing. Biking through this 60-odd kilometres of strange creations, I got lost in time.

Mexican Hat was the first checkpoint in Utah. I had my first sleep before this, but it wasn't a very good sleep, really. I couldn't settle into it, then it felt like was over before it had begun.

Gavin went to work on the bike while I slept. I didn't change gears very often, so this would sometimes create little niggles. He'd check the chain hadn't been stretched too much and give the bike a general clean-up. That saves a little bit of weight. I'd had a bit of trouble holding onto the handlebars at one point, so it needed some extra padding. I looked at photos later and wondered what this padding was on the bars. Gavin explained that I'd asked for it. The gaps were starting to appear in my memory already. Some events are vivid and others I've had to piece together from other's recollections. That's enduro for you.

I got up and went for another 12 hours or so.

We rode on through to the aptly named Mexican Hat. This tiny settlement has an extraordinary, Monument Valley-style stack of rocks. And at the very top of this is a formation like a sombrero turned upside down, so that it is resting on the crown of the hat and the brim spread out.

And beyond this are huge, stripy cliff faces in different colours. From there and all the way through it was amazing, a stunning place – one cliff face after another, and I couldn't see where the road went. I'd drop down into one place, then go back up again.

As before, the roads were concrete through here. With sleep deprivation, my perception of things was warped and altered. I couldn't always tell the depth of the cracks in the road. Sometimes these would appear enormous, and sometimes the road rose like a brick wall coming up at me. I'd brake. Then a voice in my ear would ask, 'What are you doing?' and I'd snap out of it and start pedalling again.

I was pedalling into more climbing – and into the most joyous part of the race. And then into the agony of Kansas.

Chapter 10

Rocky Mountain High

It was like a scene out of an episode of *Monty Python's Flying Circus* – a man seated in a camping chair almost naked, just in his underpants, a straw hat and sunglasses. Dion. We were in Colorado and this was a chilly morning. I was rugged up against the cold as I passed him sitting on the side of the road.

Dion made another surprise appearance later on as we made our way across the Colorado Plateau and toward the Rockies, this time on the back of a huge iron sculpture of a stag. Ride 'em, Dion! These sorts of sculptures were at the side of the driveways of quite a few Colorado properties. There were sculptures of horses, old cowboys, and one of a bison and a lion.

There was little time for such hijinks but Dion managed to squeeze them in. The tiny size of the crew was beginning to wear the organisational side of our race campaign thin. Sleep, especially, was becoming problematic. No one had slept for the first 24 hours. Not me or the crew. This went on. After a couple of days, I got some sleep in Utah. Michelle didn't. She'd been keeping the show rolling along. She was now well into her fourth day without this essential rest. The excitement of being in the race had kept everyone awake for that first day. This hindered the prospect of the crew getting into a routine, something they would pay for later in the race.

On the bright side for me, after my uncertain start and the grinding stretches of road through Arizona, followed by the unexpected magnificence of Monument Valley, I was coming into one of the most uplifting parts of the race. Literally uplifting. It was the long climb into the Colorado Rockies and the highest point of the race at 3309 metres. This was Wolf Creek Pass through the San Juan Mountains. The entire race had an accumulated climb of 52,000 metres, but this was the biggie amongst all the hill climbs.

Before I hit this monster, there were what the RAAM route book described as 'warm-up climbs'. These were Mancos Hill, Hesperus Hill, and Baldy Mountain, so called because of the lack of vegetation on its summit. They followed the line of the Old Spanish Trail, a trading route for packmules that used paths established by Native Americans.

I loved these climbs into the Rockies. They lived up to their reputation for exceptional beauty. The warm-up climbs were themselves not insubstantial.

Hesperus Hill rose to 2565 metres. Not far over the summit was a major ski village – it was like being in the middle of Europe. I could see the appeal of skiing in this gorgeous place.

The downhill from Hesperus Hill zig-zagged down in a series of sharp switchbacks. I was going perhaps 60 or 70 kilometres an hour on a lot of approaches to these 180-degree turns. Gavin was in the follow vehicle, and he later told me he kept thinking, 'I hope he makes it around that corner.' And at the next one, he'd be thinking exactly the same thing. The crew couldn't always judge the depth of my tiredness and these turns were tight. Then he'd see me swing around the corner, missing the guardrail by a whisker. I can't have been that sleepy.

I started the climb to Wolf Creek Pass at midday. There was a reason that John Denver wrote *Rocky Mountain High* about Colorado. The Rockies make you high in both senses of the word, taking you to the top of the world amidst thrilling beauty. This was New Zealand's Southern Alps on steroids. As I climbed up to this pass, waterfalls shot out from cliff tops and between immense clefts of rock, firing cascades over the trees below. The steep valleys below razor-sharp ridges were thickly populated with Douglas firs and Ponderosa pines – they reminded me a bit of the pine forests of home except these, of course, were native to here.

Another difference was that these peaks and gullies seemed ancient compared to the New Zealand landscape, which often feels freshly minted. It seemed that the slice and grind of glaciers and the weathering of wind and water had been shaping these facades and valleys for eons.

I felt the best I had since the beginning of the race. It was a stunning climb. The air was crisp and sweetly scented with the resin from the conifers. Rivers swollen with snow melt rushed down from the peaks. Every so often, there were signs warning of elk. The road wound on upward through saddles and past fractured grey-stone bluffs.

The air here was still dry and harsh on the sinuses, so we continued lubricating our nostrils with the magic glycerine. This climb went on for hours. Hard as it was, I couldn't have loved it more. The further up we went, the cooler it got. Snow appeared between the trees and in clumps in the rivers. And the mountains, of course, were capped with bright white. For the first time in the race I needed to put on extra clothes to keep warm. It was actually getting really cold.

This climb up Wolf Creek Pass also took us to the Great Divide. This line across the high points of the Rockies marks the boundary separating two principal watersheds. On the side we were climbing, the catchments and rivers would take water to the Pacific Ocean. On the other side, water would flow in tributaries to the Atlantic.

As I made my way up this climb, my cadence was fluid and, even though I was well into the race, I felt full of heart. The beautiful scenery and the cooling air must have helped. I was down on my aero bars and I was digging in.

I might have been getting a bit carried away with my output because as I was having a crack at chasing down a rider in front of me I got really light-headed and, for a time, thought I was going to faint. I was climbing as hard as I could. The altitude may have had an effect too. I had to lighten the pace a little but the enjoyment continued. I felt fantastic on that climb.

I didn't pause at the top – it was very cold. I rolled onto the massive downhill that came afterward. The downhill there was nice and smooth with wide roads. I could fly along.

I was unaware of it at the time but after the excitement of driving up Wolf Creek Pass, Gavin found himself incredibly tired. The downhill for him was an anti-climax. He shut off and started to fall asleep at the wheel of the follow vehicle. Michelle was with him. She hadn't slept for four days, but needed to take over the driving. She slept through two time stations after this. Dion, too, slept for some time.

Apparently everyone had an episode like this. Dion almost dozed off at the wheel. And Gavin got George to drive once when he was flagging, but two minutes after she'd taken the wheel, she said she wasn't capable of driving either. Luckily, a micro break and an energy drink was enough to rejuvenate Gavin and he took the wheel for another couple of hours. The crew were stoic. But the dangers were real. One team during the RAAM rolled their RV. No one was hurt, but they had to get another vehicle to continue.

Max more than once had said that he considered following a rider in a vehicle the most dangerous facet of the crew's responsibilities. Reaction time was short, they were driving on the opposite side of the road, they may be holding up traffic, and if, for some reason, the follow vehicle driver gets distracted and the rider in front of them falls over . . .

欼

I found that when we stopped for sock changes I would rummage in the melting ice in the chilly bin, checking out what food there was. This was a bit of a preoccupation. It wasn't as if the crew was eating anything different than me. But, on the other hand, they may have missed something. I don't know. I was rummaging in there, anyway.

There was a bit of a routine we went through when I stopped. When we remembered, which wasn't always, I was weighed and had my blood glucose levels tested. Weight was the key indicator of my health through this event, and measured both hydration and nutrition. (A 2 per cent reduction in weight due to dehydration equalled a 20 per cent drop in brain power and performance. In theory, I should be the same weight at the end of the race as I was at the beginning.)

Then I'd plonk down in a chair, put my feet up, get a rubdown, a wash, and have a drink – root beers were the flavour of the day. I couldn't get enough of this tasty soft drink.

Max tried to ensure that whenever I sat down, I had my legs up. At no time were my feet to be lower than my knees and my knees lower than my hips. When I got off the bike, it was time to rest my legs, so I had to get them up. My kneecaps had now sunk beneath a couple of puffy balloons.

I found the chilly bin disappointing. But Dion was continually assuring me that I wouldn't find the spare ribs and blue crab disappointing in Maryland, at the finish of the race. Whenever my spirits were flagging, he'd bring up the prospect of those delicious morsels. It was a potent enticement. Also, I'd come up with an ad hoc rule that whenever we crossed state lines, I'd get a purple aeroplane. These soft lollies in the shape of delta-wing jets were my favourite. It was good motivation, holding out for the next state and the flight of a scrumptious purple aeroplane past my tastebuds.

As I continued on the long Colorado downhills, I was caught by some guys participating in one of the team races. They must have been zipping along because they would have started nearly a week after us, but then there were up to eight of them sharing the ride. Most of them were courteous enough to slow down and spend five minutes or so talking with me before they moved on. This was a great boost, and they showed obvious respect for a solo rider. This was a really heart-warming side of the sportsmanship of the RAAM.

We saw less of the solo riders the further we went. At the beginning of the race, we'd see the same people at big Walmart parking lots, resting or picking up ice and supplies. There would be the same buses and campervans every night. Approaching the second half of the race, we didn't see them as much – they were more spread out over the course.

The further through Colorado we went, the lower we descended and the flatter the road became. When we hit Trinidad, it was like going back into the desert. This was the beginning of the Great American Plains. Dead flat and arid, these stretch across 1100 kilometres. This is tornado country, and storms can whip up in a flash and disappear as quickly. According to the RAAM information, the weather along this stretch determines if records can be broken. A storm or a massive headwind would stifle that, whereas a tailwind might push you into the history books. Conditions might suit one rider going through, but could change for another . . .

All I knew at this point was that I wanted to eat something hot and meaty and wholesome – like a hamburger.

Dion checked the Navman and told me I was in luck. I just needed to pedal 100 kilometres beyond Trinidad, along this flat, straight road and through the heat and dust of this bare countryside, to a gleaming Burger King in a town called Kim. This was our next checkpoint. I hunkered down for the long haul to my hamburger. All I wanted was that Burger King – a Whopper and fries. No, a double Whopper. I could see it hovering before me through the heat waves. Succulent. Meaty. Cheesy. I felt like I could smell the bun. A hundred kilometres was distant, but it was going to be worth it.

A long way down this road, a car drove toward us from the opposite direction. The woman driving the car said she was 'trying to find the prison'. We'd been on the road for some time. There were no side roads, no signs, nothing that would indicate a substantial structure of any kind. There might have been a prison in miniature, something to house felonious scorpions. She looked sceptical about our lack of knowledge of the local slammer and drove off.

It seemed to take forever to get to Kim. Once we got there, however, I wasn't disappointed – I was devastated. Not only was there no Burger King, there was very little of anything: three silos, a church, four houses and tumbleweed. I asked Dion, 'Where's Burger King?' and he said, 'Dude, they must be planning that for the year 2040.' I could tell he felt bad, but I'm sure I felt worse.

The one shop there, The Outpost, was closed, despite it being the middle of the day. I consoled myself with a root beer – I was slurping down at least one of these each stop. It was hot and dry there, with a light wind drying things further. The cold, fizzy drink was a delight.

The lack of a Burger King was one problem – the lack of cellphone reception was a bigger problem. We were supposed to do a check-in here. The RAAM rules stipulate that you need to go to the checkpoints, but that you always have to ring in every six hours regardless. The checkpoints are more accurately termed 'time stations'. Michelle looked around for a public phone. She found one, but it was broken. Just as she discovered this, an old guy walked around a corner and said helpfully, 'We don't have any working telephones here.'

The crew contacted RAAM headquarters at the next time station. We got a warning for failing to do the time check. We'd already received one warning. This was because we had been over six hours between ring-ins. Michelle had thought this rule referred to six hours on the bike. I was sleeping, and we had stopped. But, of course, it didn't matter if I was sleeping. The crew started to write up a sheet in the car showing the last time they rang in, so they'd know when the next six hours had elapsed.

In Kim, Gavin said that he'd seen one kid walking to church. When the kid saw Gavin, he ran away. We were like aliens. It seemed to be an odd place for a checkpoint, but you'd need to have them every 50 to 100 kilometres for the time-station idea to work.

Time checks were necessary for the race organisers to know where all the riders were, and more importantly to know that they were all okay. There's so much sleep deprivation for the crew and the riders, it's crucial to keep track of everybody. Also, people watching on the internet can follow the racers, tracking them from time station to time station. Time checks were also used to award the in-race prizes for things like the three fastest flat sections or the three fastest hill climbs.

I didn't use the time-trial bike much, but did so going out of Kim. We hadn't encountered huge headwinds, and we were going into uniformly flat country, which should've been ideal to muscle up on the big gears of this sort of bike.

I had this quite bizarre issue, however – I could feel my gut when I bent over. It was bloated and swollen, in competition with my knees. My stomach was round like a soccer ball. Michelle and Max discussed this. Max asked, 'Does he burp?' and Michelle said, 'He's not a burper.'

'He needs to fart, then.'

'But he's not doing that, either. He's not getting rid of the gas from the root beer.'

Michelle said that the soft drink needed to be banned from the race diet. Other team members pointed out that root beer was all I wanted, that I hung out for this at every stop. Michelle was adamant. She laid down an edict: NO MORE ROOT BEER.

This was cruel and unusual punishment. First, no Burger King and now a ban on my favourite soft drink. I'd gained a liking for this while in Oceanside. It's funny how I would become fixated on some things. In the PBP, it was Orangina, a drink like Fanta. That didn't seem to have any negative effects, however.

I rode on, stewing on this a bit. But they were right. A day after the root beer ban, my stomach had flattened back to normal.

If I'd thought Arizona had been unrelentingly long, the Great Plains were a step up again. There were vast blue skies with vast, level stretches of land beneath, and dead straight roads that disappeared into infinity. This was going to be a long ride.

A couple of times during the race the RAAM media team came alongside to get an interview. They'd pull up to the follow vehicle first and ask if they could talk to me. Invariably, Gavin and George would be following. Gavin would enthusiastically agree to this. As soon as the camera crew pulled away to talk to me, he'd be onto the microphone to my earpiece. 'The hottie on the camera crew wants to interview you again. Make sure your hair's looking good and your glasses frames are outside of your helmet straps – it's more comfortable and it's what all the pros do. Very important. Make sure you zip up your top.'

Meanwhile, the camera crew would be interviewing me, asking the usual sort of questions. I would try to answer these while Gavin was in my ear, having great sport. 'Don't smile too broadly – we think there's a bit of spinach in your teeth from last night's dinner. You should've brushed your teeth. Hope your breath's okay.' I could feel them guffawing in the car behind me.

After the vivid beauty of the Rockies, the plains stretched out in a grim monotone of tedium. Not quite halfway and I slogged for every metre of gain. Gavin gave me his MP3 player with the headphones – it was wonderful. I could feel my pace pick up.

Michelle found out about this the next morning, that Gavin had put both earpieces in my ears. She was none too pleased. Riders were allowed to put in one earpiece, but not both. She was understandably upset. Apparently I needed one ear free to hear cars or other noises that might be important. And breaking such rules can incur time penalties from RAAM officials.

The names of many of the places we passed through felt very familiar – locations from films, songs and TV shows. In the last couple of days we'd passed through Montezuma Creek in Utah, and through to Cortez, Colorado. Coming up, we'd skirt past Wichita in Kansas, the next state.

In 2009 a solo woman rider, Janet Christensen, put on riding shoes decorated with red sequins in imitation of Dorothy's ruby shoes in *The Wizard of Oz*. These would return the young heroine of the movie back home, to Kansas. I was soon to discover that I'd want some sort of special footwear not to take me back to Kansas, but to take me away from that state and the bottomless hole I found myself descending into there.

Chapter 11

From killer winds to delirium

It was the wind sawing into me that crushed my spirit. We'd left Colorado. Not that you'd know. There was a sign announcing the State of Kansas, there were grain elevators and silos, then the same flat country continued, mile upon mile. Long and empty. The wind hadn't kicked in yet. But we knew as we went across the huge plains and toward the Appalachian Mountains on the other side that we were heading into potentially dangerous tornado country. The crew kept an eye on the weather.

We were going toward checkpoints in Greensburg, Pratt, Maize, which is not far from Wichita, and up to El Dorado in Kansas. Greensburg was an example of how violent the weather could get there. In 2007 the town was hit by a massive tornado, estimated to be almost three kilometres wide – wider than the town itself. The place was ripped apart. Photos of the aftermath look as though an atomic bomb had been dropped. Some 95 per cent of the town was destroyed, and the other 5 per cent was severely damaged. Eleven people died. The death toll would have been greater, but the town received a tornado warning prior to this mega-weather event hitting.

I couldn't pinpoint exactly where along the journey through Kansas the wind kicked in, but it did. Not a headwind, but a side wind – a sawing, nagging wind broadsiding me. I had to angle the bike into it, to lean over against its hot breath. It just didn't stop. It made me shitty. I snapped at the crew. Nothing felt good.

This sort of riding is horrible. You've got to lock up one side of your body and hold it there. When I passed the occasional stand of trees, the wind would suddenly die and I had to instantly adjust. Then when I'd passed that, the wind started again. And I'd have to lean over, and hold that awful position and pedal forward. This made for agonising progress. The focus required, along with the unnatural body position, was like concentrating on pain and boredom at the same time.

We stopped at a time station in Pratt called Starvin' Marvin's BBQ. This diner claims to have the best barbecue in Kansas. Riders ate for free and there was free bottled water – support crew got a generous discount on the meals. But even delicious pulled pork couldn't lift my spirits. The staff there was very friendly, and it was another example of the network across the States that boosted RAAM riders – a little-known race, but enthusiastically supported by those who did know about it.

I reluctantly got back on my bike and started into the aggravating, annoying wind. I felt like I was crabbing along, holding that angle, and the wind was a provoking, sneering presence, poking fun, goading. I began to dislike the race. Nothing about this was fun. When we passed through the small towns, all I wanted to know from the crew was 'right' or 'left'.

Sometimes I'd get detailed instructions through the earpiece, lists of things to look for when I needed to change direction. I didn't want a whole spiel. Max was the worst offender. Because he was nervous about navigating, he would give me too much information. I didn't want to know the whole manual! Just, 'Turn left at the next corner'. That sort of thing. The crew's comments in my earpiece became totally irritating. I flicked the earpiece out. They'd have to direct me low-tech, by shouting out of the window of the follow vehicle.

Just beyond Pratt, we hit the halfway point in the race.

I started to think that someone must have been responsible for this situation. The race organisers had planned the whole thing. After all, they were the ones who made up the route. Why the hell were they putting me through this? It was inhumane. I wondered what sort of cruelty existed in their hearts to do this to a person.

This sort of paranoid, irrational thinking was a symptom of fatigue. As fatigue turned into exhaustion, irrational thoughts would turn into full-blown hallucinations.

The wind was a killer. It was eating away at my energy, sapping my willpower. After the fiery trial of the desert,

I didn't expect the flat stretches of Kansas to tax me like that. That this environmental element would affect me in such a dramatic fashion was a surprise. Living in Wellington, you look out for gusting winds – howling southerly gales that come at you like a freight train, blustery northerlies that eddy wildly around you. These can take you by surprise, throw you off your bike or bump you into a car. How hard could a constant, predictable wind be? The answer is, 'Hard. Very hard.'

I limped along at a forlorn pace. The wind was pushing around the edges of me and slowly wearing me down like I was a piece of sandstone, flaking off little grains, but not so much my physical self as my spirit. I was becoming smaller and smaller as the wind cut across me. I was being worn down to the core, to the essential centre. And soon that would be gone – I'd be so diminished there would be nothing left.

I kept on going and the killer wind kept on going, hollowing me out. I rode crookedly on, loathing the state. How could anybody have fond feelings for a place like this?

As it happened, the only other Kiwi rider in the RAAM, Ron Skelton, found Kansas to be a blessing. While I battled the wind that cut across me sideways, he followed 24 hours later and got a tailwind that nudged him along through the state.

There was a bit of rolling country after this but the wind continued unabated. We passed through Cairo, Cunningham, Calista, Kingman, Colwich, to Maize, across the Arkansas River and the Little Arkansas River, Rosalia, Burnt Creek, Reece, Eureka, Neal, Batesville and Yates Center. From there was a straight run of 95 kilometres without turns to the last time check in Kansas at Fort Scott.

Fort Scott itself turned out not to be such a straight run navigationally. This is when tiredness and a little misunderstanding with language across cultures can get you in a pickle – or even lost. We had to find Route 69. The RAAM route book indicated a turn in front of a 'gas station'. The RAAM route book is very detailed, with towns, cities, villages, rivers, turns, signposts, significant landmarks and the like located in increments of a tenth of a mile (160 metres). It became obvious we'd overshot the turn into Route 69. We had to double back. This was not a simple matter as, for safety reasons, I wasn't allowed to do a U-turn. Doing an ill-advised U-turn had caused a RAAM team rider to lose his life in 2003.

I had to be bundled into the follow vehicle along with my bike, and we had to drive back to the point where we'd lost our way and pick up from there. What had happened on this occasion was that Max, who was navigating, rather than looking for a petrol station was looking for a big tank for Liquefied Petroleum Gas (LPG) – a 'gas station'. This wasn't evident anywhere.

There's pressure on the navigator – they've got the cyclist in front of them, whom they're trying to direct, there's traffic everywhere in the bigger towns and cities, and this is made worse at night when visual cues disappear. On another occasion, we were looking for a turnpike but couldn't find the right one. Again we had to double back. The problem this time was down to the street signs in America being hung on wires above intersections. These became difficult to locate at night – especially if you were looking at ground level . . .

I think everybody on the crew had an incident where they were thrown by the navigation. This can be down to something very straightforward, like not turning a page. At one checkpoint, Gavin took over navigating from George. He didn't turn the page and began giving the directions to get to the checkpoint we were just leaving. So we did all these turns and we got to a dead-end street. That was a simple lack of communication – and the effects of fatigue on the crew.

There were a couple of times when the campervan would scout ahead and suss out the route through a town. We'd follow the campervan, and this would save a bit of time and it felt safer than trying to work it out as we went. We never got majorly lost, but a few wrong turns and back-tracks can add hours to your time.

I usually like riding at night. You cycle into this narrow tunnel of light and the road seems to be moving toward you. There's something almost meditative about it. You're in your own little bubble travelling through the world.

It's a little different when you've had just a scant few hours of sleep in over five days on the road. Then it's the worst time. This is when the hallucinations – the dark hallucinations – take hold. I suspect that the lack of daylight on your body has something to do with this. The hallucinations aren't so bad in the daytime.

At night, everything is telling your body to shut down, to rest, to sleep. It becomes a nightmare. The lights from the follow vehicle throw jagged shadows on the road. Things start moving at the edge of your vision, strange things flitting about.

The nightly horror show hit full throttle after we'd entered Missouri. The dry Kansas plains gave way to lush, rolling hills and farmland. The roads narrowed, there were short sharp climbs, tight bends, then the countryside would open out again. By this time, I was wiped out as much from the wind as I was from the effort of cycling. I felt like a boxer just stepping out of the ring, punch-drunk with exhaustion, bruised to the bone.

It was my perception that it was the moistness, the damp environment in Missouri that somehow sparked what would become increasingly wild visions. The wetness in the trees and grass, the damp shadows, started to come alive.

During the RAAM briefing they'd warned us about snakes. If you ran over one of these it could fold in half and wrap around the wheel rim and flip you over. There had been cycling crashes due to these creatures crossing the road. I was surprised to see white snakes on the road, however – weren't most snakes brown or green? They started wriggling and turning, then slithering and twisting into my path. I swerved. I turned the wheel again to avoid more snakes. They twisted like white eels, aiming for my bike.

I asked the crew about the snakes – they were just coming one after the other. 'It's the white line, Josh.' Max's soft, reassuring voice came through my earpiece. (I'd stuck this back in, and would generally use it when we went through towns.)

'Take another look. It's just the white line, the centre line, coming regularly.'

I tried to readjust my vision, to rethink this. It could be the broken white line. It was hard to tell.

And then there were the dead frogs littering the road. I kept scanning them looking for a live one. Gavin, this time, asked what I was doing. I explained about the frogs and asked if they'd seen any live ones. He said, 'Sorry, we haven't seen a dead one yet.'

I was able to shake this off at the next break, the next sock change and weigh-in. We did this near a Walmart. Gavin has a photo of this. I'm looking worse for wear, face puffy and red, bags under my eyes. The follow vehicle is parked in a disabled carpark. It was the wee hours of the morning, so the need for the park was unlikely, and I was close to being disabled anyway.

The onset of the hallucinations was a sign of mental and physical deterioration.

Michelle described me as becoming child-like at this time, following crew members around and not wanting to be alone. I'd play with my food. If I heard activity, I'd toddle over and see what was happening. The body closes down and the mind closes down. The organism goes into preservation mode. You mentally regress.

Events may have become a bit of a blur but I do remember some of the strange things that happened. And some very exciting events.

Further into Missouri we saw clouds swirling all around us. They seemed to be on the horizon wherever we looked, as though we were at the centre of a giant weather system.

We pushed on, but could see this thing both ahead of us and chasing us, clouds boiling around as if somebody had hit the fast-forward button on them. The stars vanished as the sky darkened. This front was looming up at our backs, breathing down our necks, about to overtake.

Then before us, a bright oasis appeared in Jefferson, a beacon of deliverance: Burger King. We stopped in the carpark. Max went about putting my bike in the campervan and just after I had walked the 20 metres to the door, the rain burst down. It was more like a solid wall of water than rain. The van was invisible behind the deluge. When Max came in, I had my feet up and a hamburger in my hand. He was soaked to the bone.

The forecast said that this storm would pass in an hour or two. This seemed unlikely. Being from New Zealand, the expectation was that it would be there for a week. We ate our food, the crew set the alarm and I got some sleep while brilliant flashes lit up the windows, thunder crashed, rain lashed down.

An hour later when we woke, the storm still buffeted the RV. Several other RVs and race vehicles were parked in the same carpark. We decided that we would push on regardless of the weather. It was wind and rain, so what? At least it wasn't cold.

I got on the bike and rode, and over the course of the evening the storm passed over the top of us and we followed in its trail. It was a spectacular evening. As exhausted and on the edges of reality as I was, the storm was a captivating sight. I could see it before me, explosions of light illuminating the landscape. Bright, jagged veins would traverse the sky. Then, in the following darkness, fireflies would dance and flicker in the bushes beside the road like sparks left behind by the lightning strikes. Then there would be another flash, impossibly bright, and a crooked stalk of lightning would hit the ground. Then darkness, and the fireflies dipping and curving in the air. This seemed to go on the whole night. The lightning cracked open the darkness at least once a minute. It was an awesome light display, like a huge theatrical event that took up the enormous Missouri sky.

There was a group of five racers in front of us. We knew this because of our occasional connections to the internet to see how the race was shaking down. What I would have loved to have done would have been to put some distance between the field behind us and catch that leading group. If we'd been a little more vigilant with the internet, we may have been able to achieve at least part of this goal.

We didn't know it at the time, but behind us trees had fallen in the storm and blocked the road. It was lucky we left the Burger King when we did, otherwise we would have been stuck behind this obstacle for four hours waiting for the road to be cleared. We found out what had happened at later time stations – we just didn't have enough crew to watch the computer all the time, and our internet connection was dodgy at best.

If we'd known, the crew would have urged me to put in a burst at that time. Someone else's misfortune could have become my advantage. That's racing. And the knowledge of the hold-up would have spurred my competitive spirit into action. Exhausted, hallucinating, bashed by the wind, I would have dragged something out of the depths of my being – I would have ridden on pure heart. But we didn't know, and I continued to struggle with my demons, to wrestle them on the road.

The follow vehicle was throwing out its weird shadows before me. This was a blacktop part of the road – presumably it had been repaired with bitumen. This is where I saw people trapped beneath the asphalt, trying to haul their way out. These people were clawing and moaning to escape. They looked to me as the only one who could help them. I didn't even know how to help myself. They must have been dying down there, suffocating. Or they were already dead, corpses from the underworld, zombies who only knew pain and dread and need.

I told myself that they weren't there, that this wasn't real. Just keep cycling, push on through it. The horror show continued, terrifying things, the worst visions attacking every effort, each pedal stroke, the breath going in and out of my lungs.

It is little wonder my memory has faded in and out for the next couple of states – who would want to recall these vivid, painful visions of suffering? In a very real way, I was looking at my own suffering. I was the one projecting these macabre images onto the road. They were coming from my mind and therefore my perception of what was happening to me.

Some of what follows I've pieced together from what the crew have told me. And every so often, something will trigger a memory and another part of the race comes back to me – a bright piece of the mosaic of this mad event falls into place and the picture becomes more complete.

Chapter 12

Rocky road to Indiana

'If I'd known it would be like this, I would have brought my mountain bike.' I was grumbling as we bumped over miles of roadworks in Illinois.

We'd come down into the Missouri Valley, crossing the Missouri River twice, then after some little climbs we descended into the Mississippi River Valley. The approaches to the Mississippi River had, on one side, these stratified cliffs of beautiful, bone-white stone with small trees below, and the river on the other. We crossed the mighty Mississippi at Alton and into Illinois not long after sunrise.

The river was in flood. This body of water would have been an amazing sight even at its normal flow. It was like passing over a firth it was so wide. And with the extra volume of water coursing through it, the river stretched out to its flood plains, making it even wider. There were wild muddy channels and turbulent swirls over its surface. The bridge we crossed is a remarkable structure. The Clark Bridge has two pylons that rise high above it and hold the span up in two 'tents' of cables wrapped in yellow plastic.

I crossed the Mississippi after six days and 14 hours of cycling. There were only a couple of time stations in Illinois. Although I remained aware of the direction and route I needed to travel, I was often in another realm. Daytime was better than the nights, however. The strange images retreated back to the shadows, waiting for when night would fall before they invaded my vision again.

I was wrecked from days on the bike and the Kansas wind. Despite this, from Greenville to Effingham, Illinois, I had my third-fastest average speed between time stations at 17.93 miles per hour (28.86 kilometres per hour). The fastest had been from South Fork to Alamosa, Colorado, which was 23.3 miles per hour (37.5 kilometres per hour) and was comprised of a gradual downhill all the way. The second fastest had been in the first part of the race, between Lake Henshaw and Brawley, which had the downhill of the 'glass elevator'.

Getting a speedy run on the flat was a welcome boost, given I was sleep-riding. My eyes were open, my legs were pushing, the wheels were turning, and the entire world around me was like a movie in progress – rolling around, real but not real. The Illinois landscape passed me by, neat farmland, maize fields, lightly rolling country, a colourful travelogue in progress.

This pleasant tourist view of the state changed when we hit roadworks. The workers there had this machine that lifted the top off the road, leaving this rough surface, all ripples, bumps and ridges. These vibrated up through my wheels into my hands and arms, then shuddered up through my legs. Every so often I'd jolt into a deeper rut, and the rumba continued, a frenetic rhythm shaking up through the carbon-fibre of my bike. It had no shock absorbers, hence my grizzle about needing a mountain bike for this terrain.

This went on for miles. I asked Dion and George if we were going the right way. 'They can't put us through this,' I told them. They were sympathetic, saying it was bad enough in the follow vehicle, it must be awful on the bike. They were sure we were on the right route but double-checked the route book, just in case.

Strict protocols had developed with the route book in the follow vehicle. All turns had been highlighted so they wouldn't be missed. The last time-station check-in was recorded at the top of the page so that we wouldn't go six hours without calling into RAAM headquarters. The odometer was reset at each time station. This was marked at the top of the page and the bottom of the page – essentially it was zeroed and checked twice: when the team rang in or went into the checkpoint, and when the team started out in the next section of the race.

This was done so that the precise measurements in the route book could be followed exactly. If the support crew missed out zeroing the odometer, they then had to subtract what they had on the odometer and match this up with the route measurements. A complicated procedure when your brain is in a fog of sleep deprivation. This was also true for the RV, which often followed different routes. On occasions when this vehicle had to take a detour, to get petrol for example, then this arithmetic had to been employed to stay on course.

Dion assured me that we were on the right road, as far as he could tell. There was a fair bit of faith put into the route book. It was our RAAM bible. And we just had to trust it was taking us along the right path.

The road rumbled on, dusty and gritty. It was a hot, uncomfortable ride. I began to feel my muscles again. The vibrations through my body made me realise how much everything ached. My chest hurt and my hands and wrists hurt. The movement rattled up into my back. How long would these roadworks last? I couldn't see the end of them, but then the road wasn't like the long straights of Arizona and Kansas. I'd go over a small rise and the broken surface continued. I'd round a slight bend and there was the same scraped surface.

There was more than 35 kilometres of these roadworks in the end – the Americans never do things by halves. My bones had been shaken up and my innards felt like a gurgling mud pool. I was sure the support crew was right, that we were on the right track, and I wondered how this had gotten into the route. Perhaps this section of road had been torn up after the route had been finalised? It was the only explanation I could come up with.

It was a miracle that we didn't get more punctures – there was only two in the whole race. Only one of them was mine. Gavin would be at my bike whenever I slept, changing tyres, checking things over, always making sure it was in superb condition. The follow vehicle got the other puncture. It was surprising that there weren't more punctures because of all the debris on the side of the road. There were shreds of truck tyres with bits of metal sticking out of them, discarded stuff, broken glass, wheel rims, plastic containers, fast-food wrappers, bits of cars.

Two hundred and fifty kilometres and 11 hours later we were coming into Indiana, and I was entering the weird zone, the nightly show of bizarre sights. I once saw a number of giant deer on the side of the road, and an enormous stag. I later mentioned this hallucination to Dion. 'That was no hallucination, dude,' he said. 'I saw them too.'

For safety reasons, I always had to be in the lights of the follow vehicle at night. And when three cars had gathered behind us, both the follow car and I would have to pull over to let them pass. It was called 'caravaning' if you didn't – holding up traffic, in other words.

Once the vehicles passed, we could start again. A variation of the rule applied during the day – the follow vehicle had to pull over whereas I didn't. Passing cars could see me. At night, this wasn't so certain. Race officials along the route kept an eye on racers to make sure they abided by these rules. There were a couple of officials in each stage, driving back and forward. A few times, we'd see them drive by and they'd toot and wave. This was especially uplifting on long nights otherwise empty of cars.

If you were observed breaking rules, you could be subject to time penalties. At each time station we'd ask if we had any penalties. We didn't get any, although we did receive a couple of warnings. The crew had been as scrupulous as possible in following the rules and RAAM procedures. As mentioned, these were mostly concerned with safety, so there was good reason to closely adhere to them. At the end of the introduction to one section of the race in the route book, in which the potential hazards of the area had been detailed, was the sentence: 'Look out for yourself and your racer's safety as if someone's life hangs in the balance.'

The follow vehicle gets a bit of a beating in this race. A lot of the time, the vehicle has one wheel on the road and the other in the gravel and glass, along with the other detritus expelled from cars and trucks. At one point, Gavin was driving through Indiana and heard this scratching noise. It persisted for some time and eventually he mustered the energy to investigate it. He looked out the window to discover the car had been dragging a large branch for the last 30 kilometres.

No one was getting enough sleep. The original idea had been that when I was asleep the crew would organise things. But we simply didn't have the numbers, so when I slept the crew slept. We were constantly scrambling. Situations would change and we'd all need to be awake.

Gavin related one time when he'd started his shift in the follow vehicle at around five o'clock at night. Max, George and he drove to midnight. I had my sleep. There was a nearby bike shop open all night, as the owners knew RAAM riders were coming through. Gavin checked this out then went to Walmart to get food. He came back, serviced the bike, but by then it was time to go again.

He jumped into the car and he and George drove to six or seven the next day. By then, he'd been awake for a 34-hour stretch. They'd take No-Doz at night and have energy drinks during the day – cold liquid to combat the heat. By the end of this spell, they were yelling at each other, 'Are you awake?' Gavin, who was driving, would say, 'Sweet. Yeah, I'm awake.' They found this yelling back and forth hilarious. So he'd yell back to her, even though she was in the passenger seat beside him, 'Are you awake?' And she would say, 'Yeah.' Then after a minute, she said, 'Did I reply to you?'

I had to have sleep. I remember saying to Gavin, 'I need a nap. Just five minutes.'

He replied, 'Are you sure? You just had a nap.'

'I definitely need a nap,' I assured him, 'I can't go on.'

'Well, don't tell Michelle that you had one,' he said.

'Thanks, Gav!' I lay down on the side of the road in the grass and as soon as I closed my eyes I was in blissful oblivion. He gave me five minutes, and I was still out to it. He gave me two more minutes. That was seven minutes. He woke me. I was grateful for the rest, got back on my bike and slowly started moving the pedals around. It must have been tough for the crew, urging, cajoling, pushing me to get going. I had told them prior to the race, 'No matter what I do, how much I protest, how tired I look, you have to tell me to go on.' They didn't have to take me seriously, did they?

I'd managed to drag myself through the previous night's strange and sometimes frightening illusions. But now everything looked weird to me. There were people on ride-on mowers, cutting lawns that weren't much bigger than sections we have in New Zealand. Very odd. They looked as though we were driving little vintage cars around the grass. Strange.

And there was one in every other house, riding their toy vintage cars.

When we got back out on the highway, I really knew I was losing my marbles. A road sign loomed up that depicted a silhouette of a horse and buggy. I should be watching out for horse-drawn vehicles? Now that's bizarre – I'm really seeing things.

It turns out that Indiana has a sizeable Amish population. These deeply religious people don't use modern technologies, such as cars. The sign was a real warning to look out for carriages towed by horses . . .

Chapter 13

Crashing in Ohio

The crew could tell from the follow vehicle that I was falling into micro-sleeps. I was doing a lot of over-correcting – going in one direction then suddenly swerving when I'd gone too far. I'd weave a bit, recover, cycle on then do it all again – jack-knifing and jerking around the road.

After leaving Indiana, there were 320 kilometres to cross Ohio. That constituted a day's riding, but my pace was as wobbly as my steering. From a respectable 28.86 kilometres per hour in Effingham, Indiana, my pace had declined over four successive time stations to 10.73 kilometres per hour on the way to Oxford, the first time station in Ohio. Admittedly there was a sleep in the last stretch, but the trend was all downwards. The crew were doing their best to keep me focused – and just keep me on the bike. Every pedal stroke was a pedal stroke closer to the finish.

They'd toot the horn or talk to me through the mic if they thought I was straying too far out into the road. There was some measure of protection from the follow vehicle – it could act as a block car, but only up to a point.

Sometimes I'd find myself spinning really fast, my legs whirring around like I was Roadrunner. I was in my lowest gear on reasonably level country, the pedals zipping up and down and me slowly moving forward. Then there was more swerving and suddenly coming-to and correcting my line.

I stopped suddenly. The voice in the earpiece asked what I was doing. I told the voice about the brick wall in front of me. 'You're all right,' came the reply. 'Keep going, keep going.'

Then lampposts started swerving in front of me and I'd have to turn sharply to dodge them. There were snakes on the road. The voice in the earpiece assured me that these were just cracks in the surface.

The pity was that this was smooth country, hot and humid, but also level and green. Often farms stretched out on either side of the road. This was where I should have been picking up my pace, as later, toward the end of Ohio and into West Virginia, the hills would start again, and after these came the Appalachian Mountains with the steepest climbs of the entire race. But I was rambling through some barely contained patches of sleep, a somnambulist cyclist.

I can only thank the combined efforts of the crew in helping me to push my speed up to over 20 kilometres per hour. I battled all day to keep my eyes open, to keep on the move. The crew kept at me, just trying to get me through to the next phase of the race, to help me find my energy and motivation again. Dion kept up his barrage of inducements.

I limped along through the day. Then at dusk, the swerving and micro-sleeps kicked in big-time again. There was an Ohio cop behind the follow vehicle, just sitting in behind at the slow pace we were doing on an otherwise empty stretch of road. I would start to doze, would wake with a jolt, over-correct my bike, swerve, then get back to some semblance of a straight-ish line. Then do it all over again. Except for the instance when I dozed a little too much, woke with a start, over-corrected the bike and went tumbling over the white line onto the wrong side of the road. Luckily, there was no oncoming traffic. I immediately thought that the cop follow-ing us would pull up and arrest me. He did pull out from behind the follow vehicle, but went around me while I was still lying on the road and took off into the distance.

I had grazed my ankle, knee, bottom and shoulder. I actually think I fell, then woke up in the middle of falling and tried to correct then. I hadn't had time to put out my hand, which was also lucky. I could easily have sprained or broken my wrist. The bike took part of the impact of the crash and I sort of rolled with it.

When the crew came rushing over to help me, I said, '*That* woke me up.' Max patched me up with the efficiency and care of a trained trauma nurse.

Michelle describes me as looking terrible when I stepped into the RV, which was stationed at a parking lot in the Ohio town of Chillicothe. I must have resembled an extra from *The Mummy*. I was wearing white cycling clothes that had been ripped and had picked up grime from the road, plus I had all these bandages wrapped around me. People from the local bike shop came in and took photographs. I'm sure they've got these framed and on the wall next to their portraits of Lance Armstrong and Eddy Merckx.

The irony was that in the crash I had ripped my expensive shorts. That actually pissed me off because I'd been wearing the cheaper ones for so long, then when I spill off my bike I've got this expensive European brand on that had a double layer of chamois.

The crash was slightly ignoble but there were worse stories. Dion told me of one rider he'd seen along the way who was covered in blood after a crash – he'd hit an armadillo.

I had no real injuries, just a couple of scrapes. I kept on going. Towards the end of Ohio, the hills started – these weren't long climbs but they were exhausting all the same. The need for sleep competed with every movement I made. I felt like I couldn't go any further.

I jerked the bike to the side of the road, braked and stopped. I dismounted, pulled off my shoes and gloves and sat down with my head between my knees. Dion and George were in the follow vehicle, and Dion jumped out, ran up and crouched down beside me. He asked me what was up. I remember saying to him, 'Dion, I ride because I enjoy it. This is killing my passion for cycling.'

Dion was sympathetic, encouraging. He talked to me for a while, asking how I would feel if I didn't finish. Those awful letters next to my name: DNF. I'd only ever pulled out of a race due to mechanical failure or to circumstances that were completely out of my control. I'd never abandoned a race because it was physically or mentally too tough. This was uncharted territory. I was out in the wilderness with this one.

I got back on the bike and struggled on. Dion had his head out of the window of the follow vehicle, shouting encouragement, promising bribes of pork spare ribs and blue crab, yelling that I was an enduro maestro. He shouted until his voice nearly gave out.

The crew checked me into the time station for Athens, Ohio at 1.17am after eight days, nine-and-a-half hours of riding.

I was getting one-and-a-half hours of sleep each night. I needed every second of this before I tackled the Appalachians.

⚬⚬⚬

The terrain eased out after Athens, a reprieve before the hard stuff to come. We crossed over the Ohio River and into West Virginia at Parksburg. The roads narrowed here and the climbs were short and sharp. There were rollers but these soon gave way to ridges, relentless steep climbs, in quick succession.

A lot of the teams catch up with the solo riders later in the race. Several passed us in West Virginia. It felt like chaos through this stretch – at least, there was chaos in my sleep-deprived brain. Then there were these pick-up trucks – big vehicles by New Zealand standards – that squeezed you as they went past. Their agitation at having to share the road with cyclists was obvious.

They'd pull up to the follow vehicle and cruise level with it while the pick-up truck driver abused whichever team members were following me. Dion, when he was driving, would reply in his laid-back way, 'Dude, we've advertised what's going on as much as possible. There's a sign saying there's a cycle race on. We're only going through this state for a day.' And then they'd pull up next to me and start shouting that I should get out of their way, that the road is made for cars, not bikes. Then they'd blow past, cutting in front of me as close as they could. I wondered if they all went to the same clothes store because they all seemed to be wearing the same style of checked shirts. I was waiting for one of them to pull out a shotgun and level it at my riding helmet. These guys were seriously angry, and more than somewhat put-out that we'd invaded their turf and interrupted by a few seconds their God-given right to rip through the mountain range. I was in a hurry, too. It was just a much slower-paced hurry.

I was digging into what resources I had left. I didn't think there were any, but I kept at these climbs. Between time stations in Grafton and Keyser, West Virginia, we dipped into Maryland for 15 kilometres then back into West Virginia.

Throughout the race, the crew had commented on how good my sense of direction was. I'd spot the route signs, and I had a nose for which was the correct turnpike or ramp. But this went strangely awry in West Virginia. We were going through a small town late at night and I started turning up people's driveways, always turning to the right. Then I'd turn back down, cycle along to the next driveway and make a right-hand turn up that one.

Michelle and Max were in the follow vehicle puzzling over this, wondering what the heck I was doing. Along came the next driveway, I'd turn right, cycle up to the garage, realise that I couldn't go through there, then pedal back again and start up the road. Right along the road of this town, I turned right up every driveway. Then when a street bisected it, I'd want to turn right down the street. Michelle yelled at me through the mic to come back.

I did, but I was convinced she had it wrong. Right was right, I was sure of it. We came out of the town and onto a motorway and there was a secondary road to the right of this. Finally! I swung right and pedalled down there. This, plainly, was the way. The road went downhill to a big Taranaki-style gate. I jumped over it.

I could hear Michelle yelling to Max, 'Get him!' They'd driven past the side road I'd pulled into and Max came belting down the road and up to the gate just as I was pulling my bike over it. He grabbed hold of the bike.

Max said to me very politely, 'Where are you going? You should be going this way.' He pointed down the road to where Michelle was backing the car up. I knew this was wrong. I'd seen a sign pointing the way to Oceanside, it was 3200 kilometres away – I just needed to turn right to get onto the correct route. Max said, 'We're going to Annapolis in Maryland.'

I didn't know what sort of stunt Max was trying to pull, but I knew where I needed to go. I told him, 'I'm going to Oceanside – you're tricking me. You're lying to me. This is the way.' He wouldn't let go of my bike. I tried to wrench it off him but he had a firm grip. It was very strange that the crew were getting it so wrong.

'I'm going back home,' I told him. 'I'm going to Oceanside.'

'You won't get anywhere that way.' He indicated the tar-sealed road behind me. It was like one of the little forestry roads you'd see in the back blocks of New Zealand, the sort of road that disappears over a hill and into nothing.

But I had seen the sign, I was certain this was the way.

Michelle drove the car toward us and we were flooded with illumination by the headlights. She walked up to me and asked, 'What are you doing, Joshua?'

I told her about the sign, about Oceanside, that we had to get onto the right track.

She calmly and firmly repeated what Max had already said: 'We're in the RAAM, Josh. On our way to Maryland. Just come over the fence. Let's talk about it.'

'You're lying,' I said. 'You're tricking me.'

'I'm not, Joshua,' she said. 'I'm trying to get you going in the right direction.'

Max now had hold of my clothes. When Michelle wasn't urging me over the gate, Max had soothing words. I didn't know what their motives were, why they would want to pull the wool over my eyes. This was absurd behaviour. I'd seen the sign. It was indisputable. Michelle's words eventually cut through my certainty. Although I felt in the pit of my stomach that I was heading the right way, that they, for whatever reason, were trying to fool me, my addled mind was telling me that Michelle was straight with me, a friend and backer, on my side.

I climbed back over the fence and we walked to the car. The familiar RAAM-related stuff in the vehicle gave me some confidence that Max and Michelle were telling the truth. I ate some aeroplane lollies – that was good. They pointed me in the direction they said I should be going. I got on my bike and started to work the pedals. It felt wrong. There was this doubt lingering in my body. I'd seen the sign and I was now cycling in the opposite direction. But I had to trust somehow. I had to believe that they were supporting me as they had for so long through the race. I cycled into the leaping shadows cast before me.

ڶ

We crossed into Cumberland, Maryland after midnight. The steepest hill climbs of the entire RAAM came between Cumberland and the time station after it, Hancock. The elevation wasn't huge, nothing like the Rockies. But the gradient was the most extreme of any of the RAAM climbs. This race had extremes in all directions and now it was *up*. I'd studied the route book in detail before the start and I knew this was going to be hard. I didn't appreciate how hard, though.

I was up out of the saddle and I could feel my heart in each downward stroke, each power movement on the pedals. I was hurting with the effort. But this was the steepest part of the ride, and if there was anything I could do on a bike, it was climb.

Michelle's voice came through my earpiece, 'Get off the brakes, Joshua. Release your hands from the brake handles. Get off the brakes, Joshua.' I realised the grunts I could hear were my own. 'Drop your gears, Joshua. Lower your gears. Get your hands off the brakes.'

I was grinding up this climb. It was to be expected that it would require some kind of effort from the pit of my guts. I gave it.

Through the earpiece Michelle was saying, 'Change your gears down. Click through the levers, first on your right hand then your left.'

Michelle ran up beside me and stopped me altogether. I was gasping for air. She clicked my gears and got me to lift the back wheel and turned the pedal with her hand. The chain slipped down over the cogs. 'Stay off the brakes, Josh. Keep the gears down here.'

I started on the climb again. And the hill got steeper and harder, more gruelling. Michelle's voice came through the earpiece, 'You've changed your gears back up, Joshua. Change them down. Click through the gears – you're on your highest gear. Change your gears down, Josh.'

I rode the steepest RAAM climb in high gear, up out of the saddle and grinding and sweating the whole way.

Despite all the odd behaviour and the effects of sleep deprivation, the crew have said that I was generally coherent during time-station check-ins, when I had my socks changed, had a wash and did the weigh-in. I knew what I wanted and what I needed from them.

What I wanted from them in the next part of the race was release. I wanted respite. I wanted to pack up my bike and go home. Solo RAAM racers usually go through this at least once in a race – and sometimes several times. Each rider experiences this differently and expresses it in their own way.

It can be a shock for the support crew to see you hit the floor. And they may not know how to react when they see you so wiped out and desperate. Their fortitude is needed to help restore their rider's motivation, to shore up mental toughness. And this is when the make-up of the crew is important – that motivator, coach, psychologist, martinet needs to be in the mix to insist, to demand, to order the racer to continue. In the end, that's what an endurance athlete wants – to make it to the finish line. And to win, of course, but you have to pass that line first.

Chapter 14

Meltdown in Maryland

I may have physically crashed in Ohio, but my average speed between time stations had crashed at the end of West Virginia and on to the first two time stations in Maryland. The steep climbs over the mountains naturally had an effect and my unique method of climbing these definitely slowed progress. But behind this drop in pace was my diving mental state, my descent into mental exhaustion.

Somehow, I made it through to the next day and to Hancock. The approach to this peaceful, green little town was through a man-made, gorge-like pass that had been gouged out of a mountain-top.

We did the time-station check-in at 7.14am. And then it was time for me to ride again. I got on my bike. But I didn't want to ride. I couldn't. I was at an end point in my mind. I'd finished. There was no more racing, no more gas in the tank, nothing left to fuel my willpower. I was wrung out and empty. It was over.

There were 290 kilometres left to go, but it may as well have been the thousands of kilometres back to Oceanside, where I'd tried to ride to the previous night. The final run to Maryland stretched out before me, an infinity of pedal strokes. This torturous last leg taunted me with its impossibility. I hated my bike. I dismounted and threw it down on the side of the road. I gave up. Locals were walking past but I didn't care. What did they know?

Max tried to talk to me. His voice was soft and understanding, soothing. It was like a meditation. His years in the caring profession, being a nurse, put a relaxing tone in his voice. I still wasn't going to do a thing, however.

I just said, over and over again, 'I'm not doing this anymore.' He kept on at me and I snapped, 'Fuck off! This is it. I'm not going on. I can't do this anymore.'

Michelle was kneeling beside me too. I think she must have had enough by now as well. She blew a fuse and started nutting off at me. 'Not riding anymore! Yes, you are!' A full-blown Kiwi domestic developed on the street of this quiet Maryland town. She was saying that all these people had put time and effort and money into me, that I had no injuries, and that I wasn't going to give up now. The rest of the crew scattered at this outburst. They left us to it.

I stayed sitting on the ground – I wasn't budging. Michelle tried to pick me up but I wasn't having that either. I resisted. She tried harder so I lay down. I made myself stiff, stretched out hard and stiff as a board. Michelle must have been really pissed off because she hooked her hands under my arms and picked me up and put me on my feet. She's petite but fit, and the anger would have given her a burst of adrenaline.

Then she picked up my bike and put it in my hands and pushed me down the road, the whole time a torrent of admonishment coming out of her mouth. We walked along, me pushing the bike and Michelle saying that I wasn't going to stop. Hancock townsfolk came up to us to see what was going on as we walked along, Michelle yelling at me the whole time. I obviously looked a mess, haggard and exhausted, morose. A fireman even approached us and asked if everything was all right. Michelle ignored him, completely cut him off. He left.

The words and anger poured out. How could I even think of giving up? We'd come this far, been through the qualifier, the training, flown to America, there was only one way I was going and that was forward. I stonewalled, repeated myself. I wasn't going any further. This was enough – too much! I wasn't going anywhere, not on a bike.

But I was. I had to. Michelle asked me what I was going to say to my grandad. She meant my grandfather on my mother's side. He keeps clippings from the racing I do. He would be keeping all the RAAM news as well. He'd given me money, and there were all the other people who'd worked their hearts out to get me there too. These words were sinking in. I look up to my grandfather. To go back and explain to him why I didn't finish – this was unpalatable. I got back on my bike, grudgingly.

According to RAAM rules, strictly speaking, a crew member couldn't walk beside me for this period of time.

We could have received a penalty for this. But Michelle had weighed that one up — a fifteen-minute penalty? Or not finish at all? As far as she was concerned we'd already wasted close to a day. We hadn't gone far and there was a 12-day limit to race completion. She wondered if it might have been better to let me sleep for another four hours. The problem was, if I'd gone into a deep sleep I mightn't have come out of it for 12 hours or even a day. I would have shut right down, and my body and mind would have lost the momentum. She made the decision at that point to not back down. She was adamant I'd continue. If she hadn't, the likelihood is that the campaign would have been over right there.

I rode on, and the anger and resentment rode with me. But the words and Michelle's implacable resolve had seeped in. The pique started to drain away. It was like there was a dammed-up pool in me that had breached and the water was flowing out. I rode for how long — perhaps 10 kilometres. What was left then, after those childish, stubborn refusals had flowed away? Remorse. Sorrow. And something else: a deep sense of appreciation of those around me, of those who'd got me there.

Me wanting to give up on the race suddenly seemed petty and selfish when all these people had helped and supported me. The crew had been with me every moment, had backed me through their own privations, sleeplessness, discomfort. And I wanted to quit on them, and all the people who'd backed me? I felt like a prick.

Dion was a good friend and I think he found it hard seeing me suffer. Our friendship went back to Monrad Intermediate, where we raced each other on the sports field.

Occasionally, he would win. And then all those mountain-bike rides and competitions, and the pizzas and hamburgers afterward. Throughout the RAAM, he had been conscious of keeping me warm and cooling me off. He'd been aware of my sensitive feet when he changed my shoes and socks. He'd been incredibly vocal, cheering me on throughout the race, clowning it up in rare free moments to lift my spirits.

His partner, George, energetic, contained – she had immediately got into the spirit of the race, had been proactive in the crew, dealing with provisions and storage without any prompting, driving the follow vehicle, navigating along with everyone else. Quietly staunch, she could always be relied upon.

Max, whom I'd met only months before, had brought his long experience as a nurse, his extensive knowledge as a traveller, to the crew. Always affable, he had also brought original ideas to the team in keeping me well, and often speculated on ways we could improve the organisation and procedures going ahead if I ever undertook this madness again.

Gavin never missed a beat with my bikes. When I was off my bike or sleeping, he worked. The cycles were always pristine and smooth to ride, excellently maintained. Gavin was also a junk-food buddy. We tucked into the frozen yoghurt and crab in Oceanside, and halfway through the race he'd found our favourite doughnut shop where he bought a mixed box of 24 of these scrumptious snacks. Cheerful and easy-going, he'd stuck with the programme with the rest.

And then there was Michelle. She'd got me there. If she hadn't been involved, I would've most likely listened to those people who said I couldn't do it, it was too expensive, a near-impossible race to finish. She was the organisational backbone to the race campaign, and took on the role of crew chief at the last minute. All the things I thought I couldn't do – or didn't know how to do – she took on and made sure that they happened. It had been hard on our relationship. We hadn't been going out long before the RAAM hit the fan. In the time when we should have been enjoying our first moments together we were organising itineraries, getting visas, fundraising, confirming crew, building up biking supplies.

Then I was crying. More than crying, I was bawling my eyes out and saying, 'Sorry, sorry, sorry.' I dropped back next to the follow vehicle and said sorry to each of the crew – to Michelle and Max. They stopped the car, and Michelle ran beside me and we hugged while I pedalled on. Then Dion, I apologised to him too, my face was awash and stinging with salt. George, Gavin, Max, I apologised to them all. To each one in turn. I wanted to apologise to each of them individually. The tears came out, sobs from the pit of my stomach. I was riding my bike and bawling like a kid.

This was some sort of breakdown, but also a breakthrough. I struggled on. The exhaustion was still there but some sort of barrier had been broken down. An obstacle in my mind had toppled and the race was back on. I might not gain any more places but I was going to finish, that was for certain. Whatever it took, I was going to make it to Annapolis. My unique race number may be 414, but I was going to be part of the smaller group of solo riders that actually finished – some 250 to date in the third decade of the race's history.

After leaving Hancock, we entered Pennsylvania. I wrestled through the last biggish climbs in the race, and then the hills moderated the further we went. I had upped the pace from the preceding time stations and was feeling clear and focused.

We went through historic covered bridges and into the Gettysburg National Historic Park. This commemorates the site of America's most famous Civil War battle. Prompted by General Robert E. Lee's second attempt to invade the North, forces of the South and North faced each other in the fields and hills of Gettysburg in the bloodiest battle of this bitter war. The place is an orderly park, with statues and monuments, Civil War cannons, and 'worm fences'. These fences are comprised of lengths of timber laid across each other. The self-supporting structure requires a zigzag pattern, giving rise to its wriggly name.

After all we'd been through in the race, grappling with wild terrain and difficult circumstances – the baking desert, the splendid Rockies, the storm on the Great Plains, the crazy drivers of the Appalachians, the last steep grinding climbs, the mind-boggling visions, the meltdown – sedately cycling through this composed park provided another contrast, a subdued and formal civility. It was hard to believe that these neatly trimmed fields of grass and gentle hills had been soaked in blood over the three days of the battle.

We continued through this green countryside and I was feeling good. The names of the roads we passed through mirrored my mood. Mount Pleasant and Grandview took us toward the next time station in Hanover. We re-entered Maryland and rolled down peaceful rural roads.

We were some way down one of these stretches of mostly unpopulated landscape when a couple appeared from a house at the side of the road. They waved at us and shouted out, 'Can you stop?'

I braked and pulled over, as did the follow vehicle. These people knew that the RAAM was coming though. They said that we were the only racers who had stopped when they'd called out. Their daughter had made chocolates and cakes especially for the RAAM riders. The young girl presented a plate of beautifully decorated sweets. They were wrapped in red, white and blue paper and had little American flags attached to them.

This more than compensated for the West Virginia pick-up truck drivers. It was a moving and humbling experience. The young girl had obviously put all this time and care into them – and I'm never one to turn away food treats.

We were on the final time stations for the race. We checked in at Mount Airy at 5.20pm. This was the last 'penalty box' of the race. All racers had to check for time penalties there, and if they had any, they were to be served at this place. We had accrued none, and moved on straight away. From Mount Airy to the official finish line was under 90 kilometres.

We continued on through the last reaches of this rural area, but the evidence of the populous centres of the States became impossible to avoid. This came in the form of enormous interstate freeways that connected Washington to New York City. We traversed these multiple-lane highways as we drew closer to Annapolis.

As the night closed in, the finish was only a few hours away.

Chapter 15

10 days 5 hours 27 minutes

It felt like we were going in a big circle, curving out and around in a circuitous arc to Annapolis. The end of the race was a strange winding down. I just wanted to finish. I'd done the race, done the hard yards, faced down my demons. I wanted to stop, find a rib-and-crab palace and chow down.

I'd pushed up my pace in anticipation of completing the journey and was in the final burst that the end of a competition often brings.

Dion and George drove the RV on an alternate route for the last part of the race, going ahead of the rest of us to the ceremonial finish line. This is because there aren't many roads that lead into the main centre of Annapolis. Its one-way streets are always busy. For safety reasons, RVs went a separate way. It meant that Dion and George could watch me come in for the final part of the race.

The official timed end to the race was at the Rams Head Roadhouse. In the parking lot of this establishment a little marquee without sides, like a gazebo, was set up with a portable table that had collapsible legs. It was rather an inauspicious conclusion – no cheering crowds, no bunch of flowers, no champagne – a typical enduro finish. My official time of arrival was 9.10pm.

From this time station, there was a cycle of a few miles to a petrol station. There we had to wait for an official RAAM vehicle to escort us to the ceremonial end of the race. This was dockside, so that the race went from ocean to ocean. Fast freeway traffic merges with the route for this last phase, so the escort vehicle was to ensure tired racers cycled the last few miles safely. It took 20 minutes or so to bike to this Shell station. We waited there for a further 15 minutes until the escort car arrived and then we were off, negotiating the traffic to the Susan G. Campbell Park at the City Dock.

There was another wait there as the RAAM people organised things for my reception. This must be the same for each rider and the teams as they come in sporadically over three days. All the effort and urgency of racing made these short delays interminable. Eventually I was called through to cycle under the race banner and into the lights of the RAAM media crew and the cheers of my team and the small group of RAAM stalwarts.

I could hear Dion tooting an air horn. Michelle, Gavin and Max, who'd been in the follow vehicle, came behind me with the New Zealand flag draped before them. Dion shouted, 'Kiwis *can* fly!', which is a slogan from Buteline, one of my sponsors. The crowd there clapped and I was invited up onto a stage under a marquee.

There were three big flat-screen monitors before the stage, and my official race time flashed up on them:

10 days 5 hours 27 minutes

Then it was straight into an interview with one of the RAAM officials. This went out over a PA so the people gathered there could hear.

He congratulated me on being the first New Zealander to complete the RAAM, which raised a cheer from the crew. He then commented that I was looking pretty good for just having finished this mammoth ride. This was true – I'd snapped out of things in Hancock and had felt much better since then – not exactly ready to do the Highland Fling, but okay. He asked if I was riding for any particular purpose or to highlight any cause. I spoke about the Cancer Society of New Zealand. He asked why this was a concern in which I was interested, and I pointed out that as a red-headed guy with fair skin I was especially susceptible to this sort of disease. We chatted for a bit longer, he shook my hand, then presented me with the RAAM medal.

There's a photo of me wearing this with a big smile on my face. As an athlete, medals and trophies are symbols of the achievement, they come to embody the essence of the experience. They're the evidence. That night I slept wearing this gong.

The team was invited onto the stage for photographs and brief interviews. Then it was time to find our hotel . . .

�🚲

We dropped off our gear at the hotel and then tried to find some food. The only supermarket we could locate was closed – it must have been past 11 o'clock by now. Here I was at the end of the race – a bona fide RAAM cycling warrior – and I couldn't even get a decent feed. We went back to the hotel, I showered and went to bed miffed.

The crew thought that I would sleep continuously for 24 hours, but I didn't – I had a normal night's sleep and got up in the morning at the time that I would usually rise. I was definitely knackered, but because I had that little sleep – a lot more than I'd been having each night of the race – I felt better than I had in days.

Physically, I wasn't in bad shape. I wasn't stiff – it's such a long race that my body had got used to the output. People thought I wouldn't be able to walk for days afterwards but I was fine. I'd lost weight – around seven kilograms – and my eyes had sunken into my head, so I must have eaten into my muscle mass and was, perhaps, a little dehydrated.

My knees had swollen up quite badly. Most people, if they saw a physio with knees inflated like mine had been, would be told to stay off their bike for a couple of months. But that wasn't an option for me. Towards the end of the race, they had started going down. And by the finish they looked better than they did when I was 5 kilometres into the event. This, I suppose, is the body learning and developing as it goes. In fact, I felt much worse after the Taupo Extreme Enduro, when I'd covered 1280 kilometres in 55 hours with ten minutes' sleep. I was sore for days after that race, drained.

I'd been so determined to smash everyone, and I did, including myself.

Even though I got up the next day and offered to help with sorting the gear, I found myself wanting to spend time alone, away from the crew. Peeling off all the sponsorship and caution stickers, sorting out all the gear – what to keep, what to throw away – packing up, dismantling the bikes, organising all the spares and clothes, the medical equipment, the personal items, this was a huge job. Then the vehicles had to be thoroughly cleaned.

Before Michelle and I took the follow vehicle back, we took it to a self-grooming place at a service station. No matter how hard we vacuumed we couldn't get it completely spick and span. The marks made by the cogs and chain of the bike when we stuffed it into the vehicle were impossible to remove.

I think I pottered for a bit while the gear was being sorted, answered questions that Gavin and Dion put to me, did a bit of packing, but there wasn't much drive in me. I kept to myself mostly until I started to adjust to not being on the bike, until I could see the crew separately as my friends, not as my lifelines, navigators, cooks and cheer squad. Once I'd eased out of that bubble of singular focus and started to walk and breathe in the ordinary world again, I found that I could spend time with them all.

The crew needed time to adjust too. Directly after the finish of the race, they were too hyped up to sleep. They went for a walk around Annapolis and found a sports stadium, empty but with all its lights on. They walked in through an open gate into this magnificent arena. The game was over but the air was still full of the electricity of competition – that must have been how they felt.

They took a couple of days to recover. Unlike mine, their first night of sleep was broken. They woke after two hours expecting that they had to do something – cook, restock the food and ice, change my socks. I expect they would have nightmares about my socks for months to come. They'd go to sleep, then wake up again two hours later.

We hit Buddy's Ribs and Crabs the next day. This was quite a touristy place but very enjoyable. Dion claims that it was only the promise of ribs and crab cakes that got me over the line.

Later, Dion, George and I went to a bottle store and stocked up on American craft beers. The hotel had a barbecue by the pool. So, in sunny Maryland, we barbecued and downed beers like good Kiwis. The people in the bottle store recommended an 'authentic' rib-and-crab-cake place in the Maryland suburbs. Michelle and I went there and the food was superb. Local knowledge is the best. We visited that place again. We found three good ice-cream shops in Annapolis and I made solid use of them.

The crew did a trip to Washington and visited the Smith-sonian and the Lincoln Memorial. Michelle and I went for a day trip to Baltimore and did a cruise on Chesapeake Bay – it was a wonderful way to de-stress.

There were two dinners at the end of RAAM. We had a choice to go to either the first or second dinner. I'd finished in time to go to the first one but decided we'd wait for Ron Skelton, the other Kiwi, to finish so that we could attend the RAAM with him and his crew.

The dinner was held in a conference centre in a hotel. George, the guy who started off each solo racer, MC-ed the evening. He took a microphone around to each table and gave the riders an opportunity to talk and thank their team.

Interesting stories emerged from these talks. There were a number of cyclists from countries who hadn't been represented in the RAAM before, including New Zealand. A two-man team from South Korea had one of their team members hospitalised during the race. When he was discharged, he re-joined his team-mate and they finished together.

One rider from Australia finished the race exactly on 12 days, to the second. Another guy finished shortly after the cut-off time. He was straight-up with the RAAM officials when he checked in at the time station. Although this officially categorised him as DNF, he was given an award for integrity at the dinner.

During this dinner, a young American rider mistook Gavin for Lance Armstrong and asked our mechanic if he could get a photo with him. The young man's mum joined them.

Ron Skelton had a crew of five as well. We sat at a table together, the two Kiwis who finished the RAAM solo and the crews that made it possible – a select group representing New Zealand. Ron looked buggered. He'd only finished the race earlier in the day. He'd had an afternoon's sleep, then came to the dinner. His crew was hammering back the beers, but Ron had a build-up of bottles he couldn't get through.

As soon as the dinner was over, all the officials left. Everyone was tired. Most of the racers and their crews drifted away too. Except for the Australians and the Irish. They were irresistibly drawn to our table as if the accumulation of Budweiser bottles had added extra gravity to it.

The night became more raucous. Dion was giving the Aussies hell, and was well into party mode. Ron had to drive his RV back to LA the next day, so he tailed off. The table looked like it might collapse into a black hole with the weight of Budweiser bottles on it by the end of the evening.

Out of 41 solo riders across all divisions, male and female, 29 finished. This was a spectacular result for the RAAM. Usually 50 per cent finished the event. To get close to 75 per cent made 2011 a golden year. The organisers put this down to the weather being the best it had ever been during the history of the race.

Some great riders came in before me. Mark Baloh, the Slovenian rider who had been a close friend and rival of the five-time RAAM winner Jure Robic, came in third at 9 days 2 hours 59 minutes. The phenomenal Austrian cyclist Christoph Strasser won the race, cracking nine days and almost breaking the solo record with a time of 8 days 8 hours 6 minutes. I came eighth in my division and tenth overall, and was the second rookie to finish. It was good – just finishing is a big achievement – but I knew I could have done better. That would have to wait until the next time. I left a lot of gear at a friend's house in Colorado, outside of

Durango at a place called the Ghost of Springs. This I can get trucked to Oceanside for when I return.

Dion and George took the RV back to LA, touring around as they went.

Max originally came to America via Thailand where he was attending a memorial service for his brother, Ian, killed in the pro-democracy riots in that country in 1992. After the RAAM, he was going to make his way to Kenya in Africa to work at a small health centre there. He'd worked at this centre on Rusinga Island on Lake Victoria 30 years ago when he'd travelled across Africa.

Gavin made his way back to New Zealand. We stayed on in Annapolis for five days before we, too, returned home.

Chapter 16

The next time

Fear. If you asked me what emotion I have in anticipating the next RAAM, that one word would sum it up. I'd been afraid before I'd done the RAAM: the distance, the terrain, the desert especially, the length of time on the bike, the sleep deprivation. Having done the race, I was right to have been afraid. The RAAM lived up to its reputation of being the hardest cycling endurance race in the world. Now having experienced this gruelling test, I fear and respect it. And I definitely want to do it again.

As soon as I finished the RAAM, I knew I could have done better. I was disappointed in myself. I wasn't disappointed in our joint effort, however. I thought we'd done amazingly well for the size of our crew, the size of our budget and our inexperience relative to the seasoned athletes and their well-resourced campaigns.

One of the biggest lessons to come out of this race is you're only as good as your crew. As they take care of your wellbeing during the race, the management of the team and resourcing takes care of their wellbeing. We were too few. Ron Skelton also had a team of five, but their approach was quite different. They took longer sleeps and paced out the length of the route to finish within the twelve days. We were there to race. Other solo riders had crews of ten and twelve. They could do proper shifts, bring in fresh people when needed.

What we had going for us in the crew was Kiwi 'make do'. New Zealanders are good travellers. We muck in. The people in my crew were unconcerned if they hadn't showered in days. They'd sleep in their clothes and wake ready to get on with the next task.

Looking back now, a crew of seven would have been ideal for our needs. That way we could have had a permanent driver for the RV. This person would be responsible for emptying the waste from the vehicle and for filling it with fuel and water. A second person would stay permanently with the RV – a dedicated cook. This person would look after getting the ice, a good supply of which is needed throughout the race, provisioning the RV, and, of course, cooking for me and the rest of the crew. I survived on energy drinks and junk food like microwaved pizzas because these were the easiest to prepare. At the start of the race, the crew bought heaps of produce but it all went mouldy. We wanted to eat healthily but that all fell by the wayside. A full-time cook would have increased the likelihood of us all getting tasty, nutritious and healthy meals.

If a cook took care of provisioning, the people in the follow vehicle wouldn't have had to scramble to buy food and ice. They could have concentrated on their tasks of driving, navigating, and handing drinks and food to me. This would have allowed for at least two people to be resting at any time.

As it turned out, we didn't get any flow. At the beginning, we had three people in the follow vehicle – a driver, a navigator and someone feeding. This meant there were only two people in the campervan – not enough to do all the chores. The people in the follow vehicle weren't sleeping enough. We cut down to two in the follow vehicle and had three in the campervan.

Juggling these various roles had also been determined by team dynamics. Who was best at what? And who worked well together? This was sorted out on the road. A larger, more structured team would have taken the guesswork out of this part of the campaign. People would have known what their roles were and when they would be rostered on and when they could rest.

Dion thought that we could have shaved perhaps 24 hours off the time if I was pushed harder. The crew needs a drill sergeant, someone who would be hard about the schedule. Michelle toughened up to this role, but none of the rest of the crew could. No one likes seeing a friend suffer. They hadn't before witnessed how this extreme marathon would affect me, and no one knew what to expect with 5000 kilometres of cycling. This was part of the problem of having such a small crew – they had to be all things to me. This was neither fair nor possible.

During the race, I developed a wilful tendency to procrastinate, to slow everything down. It took the crew half an hour to prepare me for bed, then another half an hour to get me up, and sometimes I'd drag this out to an hour. This sort of changeover needed to be snappier. Every minute on the bike was progress to the finish line, and every minute off still saw the clock ticking. I needed to eat, drink and pee while I was riding. All activity off the bike needed to be pared back to the absolute essential. I had a lot of wasted time off the bike. I could have been sleeping instead of mucking around, and this would probably have reduced the hallucinations and other effects of sleep deprivation.

After the team disintegration prior to my 2011 campaign, buy-in by each member at least six months out would be a requirement. Then there would also need to be back-up crew in place to step up in case of emergencies.

Now we know how the RAAM works, a mock ride over a weekend would be good for crew to get practical experience in driving a follow vehicle and handing out food and drinks, preferably taking into account that this will be done while driving on the right-hand side of the road.

Things such as the need for the follow vehicle to act as a block car on occasions would, at least, need to be discussed. I don't know how crew could get the experience in New Zealand of crossing over six-lane highways, however.

A couple of things I'd put on my fantasy wish list is to be able to scout the route beforehand and have a training camp in the desert, the way some of the overseas riders do.

Seven would also be a good crew size in terms of budget. Any more and another vehicle would have to be added, pushing the costs up. We under-estimated the petrol costs for the journey. Diesel RVs were difficult to find and, oddly, more expensive to rent. Even the amount of ice needed and the cost of this was a surprise.

Next time we'll be able to start sponsorship and fund-raising early because, having finished the RAAM, I'm now qualified for this race for life. The best possible situation is to have someone whose sole responsibility it is to raise cash. This would leave me with time to do things like, oh, I don't know, train perhaps.

Doing a race like this is not cheap. We cut costs wherever we could. Sometimes this wasn't desirable. It would have been good if we could have put the crew up in a hotel rather than have them sleep in the campervan at the end of the race, for example. They needed to recover, too.

We struck bad luck with fundraising because of the recession and the Canterbury earthquake. Even high-profile athletes were only attracting 20 per cent of the sponsor-ship they needed. Sponsorship was further complicated by a mismatch of exposure. New Zealand sponsors may not see much benefit in the RAAM unless they were trying to get some penetration in the United States. And media coverage of the RAAM within the States is very limited. Likewise, American sponsors wouldn't see much benefit in me showing their brands to a tiny market of four million New Zealanders.

The medical side of the campaign worked out well. I was physically in good shape at the end, despite having lost weight. The team, too, all lost weight. A dedicated cook would help with this, as would more crew. We'd taken care of medical insurance for the States before travelling. Visiting a sports doctor before we left to get advice on anti-inflammatories and analgesics was a good strategy.

Members of the crew would need to know first aid and be able to give a test for glucose levels in my blood. We'd continue the weighing procedure as a way to measure general health and hydration.

I'm delighted to say that my butt didn't get a hiding during the RAAM. I wasn't bothered with the common endurance cycling problem of chafing or saddle sores. Max's magic concoction helped with this as did good hygiene. The crew, especially Michelle, ensured that I always had a clean pair of cycling shorts ready, and that the chamois inside these always had anti-chafing cream.

We probably went with enough gear, and we had budget to buy gear over there. That we've stored what we could re-use for when I enter the RAAM again will make some savings. Gavin had organised with the spares supplier that we could return anything we didn't use, so we had more than enough spare parts for the bikes.

We had plenty of gloves, socks, shorts and tops so that there were always some clean and dry, ready for me to change. We couldn't predict at the outset that I'd opt for merino wool socks to alleviate my hot foot . . .

It took several months, perhaps six, for me to recover from the RAAM. When you cycle ten days nonstop, you will be chronically fatigued, the central nervous system will be that run down.

I tried to get back into serious cycling a little too soon afterwards. But when I had a ride, my heart wasn't in it. I bike because I love riding and endurance racing. The first big race I tried to train for after the RAAM was a four-lap race around Taupo. I couldn't get into it. I'd never had any problems in the past getting up and heading out on the bike.

Part of my training would be to get up at 3.30 to 4.00am on Saturday, and ride over the Rimutaka Hill to Martinborough, do the weekly race that's held there, then bike home. One morning I got up, had breakfast, got dressed, put on my gear, got my bike sorted out . . . then stopped. This morning ended with me crawling back into bed and saying to Michelle that I didn't really want to go.

A few weeks later, I had a race up in Manawatu. At the end of the first lap I got a puncture and broke some spokes. Usually I'm very organised with the gear I take with me, but on this occasion I had no spokes and no spare wheel. It dawned on me that I just wasn't into riding at that point.

I spoke to Silas about it. He asked, 'When was the last time you biked around the bays in the sunshine with a grin ear-to-ear, and you felt like you could just bike all day?' I thought about it and realised it was not since I trained for the RAAM. He pretty much said to me, 'I don't want to see you again until you've got that feeling back.'

I probably wasn't being honest with myself about how I felt. I was riding because I thought I should instead of wanting to.

You live another life in a race like the RAAM. The highs are higher and the lows are below the abyss. You enter other realms and experience pain like no other, as if you've plunged into a furnace. And after you've been consumed by the fire you find that you're not dead but more alive than you have ever been. You come out on top. You've won even if you're not standing on the podium. My friend Mike Searle has said that coming second just means being the first loser, and I agree with that competitive spirit. But this is different. You win if you make it through. And I had.

Acknowledgements

I am indebted to my friends and family, past and current crews, and the trainers and sponsors who have helped me over the years.

Support crews
Dianna Bassett
Jeremy Devlin
Dai Brizzel
Jeff Jewell
Cathy Wood
Darren Tracey
Christine Bassett
Des Bassett

Brad Quinn
Kay Burns
Mark Robinson
Mike Searle
Greg Hart
Shane Tindall
Phillip Beach
Robyn Pearce
Michelle Cole
Dion McKenzie
Georgina 'George' Nation
Gavin McCarthy
Max Neumegen

I would also like to thank my family at Kuratau, who stand at their gate at all hours of the night to cheer me on, and also everyone else who has cheered me on.

Special friends and supporters
Andrew and Yvette Elliston
Craig Earles
Colin 'Wal' Anderson
Douglas Mabey
Capital Cycles
Nick and Julia Dunne at Allcar Upholstery

Coach, trainers and mender
Silas Cullen, Smartcoaching
Shane Tindall, Specifics Training Group

Acknowledgements

Phillip Beach, osteopath and acupuncturist
Brad Quinn, personal trainer

Sponsors
Searletech
Buteline
Cycletech, Louis Garneau
City Fitness, Johnsonville
Hammer Nutrition New Zealand
Aspiring Cycle Wear
My nan and grandad, Ray and Beverly Marshall
Waterwise, Jan and Karina
Craig McCleod
New Zealand Cancer Society
Tim 'The Potato Guy'
Dave Pohe

Special thanks to Michelle Cole and Dianna Bassett, who have put up with so much more than anyone probably should. Endurance racing is such a selfish and time-consuming sport, I will be forever indebted to them both for their time, patience and belief in me. I cannot thank them enough.

About the authors

Josh Kench is an ordinary Kiwi bloke who works as a plumber in Wellington by day. Nights and weekends see him out on his bike riding very long distances for fun.

Kerry Jimson was one of the brains behind the New Zealand TV shows *Skitz* and *Public Eye*, and was the senior writer for New Zealand's national museum when it opened in 1998. He now works as a freelance writer and museum consultant in Wellington. This is his first book.